AGNIESZKA WOLIŃSKA-SKUZA

THE ART OF CHANGING YOUR MINDSET

ACHIEVE INNER BALANCE AND EXCEL IN BUSINESS AND LIFE

The Art of Changing Your Mindset:
Achieve Inner Balance and Excel in Business and Life

First published by MasConsulting Art & Business in 2021

www.awolinskaskuza.com

Copyright ©Agnieszka Wolińska-Skuza, 2021

Agnieszka has asserted her right under the Copyright, Designs and Patents Act 1988 to be identified as the author of this work

All rights reserved. No part of this publication may be reproduced, in any form or by any means, without permission from the publisher

Paperback: 978-1-7397578-0-9

eBook: 978-1-7397578-1-6

CONTENTS

Preface	1
Introduction	9
How to Use this Book	23
Chapter 1: Honing Your Life Vision	29
Chapter 2: Reaching Beyond Your Comfort Zone	49
Chapter 3: Boosting Your Creativity	67
Chapter 4: Maximizing Your Productivity and Energy	89
Chapter 5: Nurturing Your Relationships	111
Chapter 6: Building a Meaningful Career	131
Chapter 7: Becoming More Resilient Against Stress	153
Chapter 8: Taking Control of Your Health and Well-being	175
Chapter 9: Embracing Spiritual life	199
Chapter 10: Expanding Your Intellectual Capacity	219
Chapter 11: Planning Financial Freedom	237
Chapter 12: Improving Your Quality of Life	257
Afterword	275
Special Acknowledgments	288
About the Author	291

This book is dedicated to my daughters, Laura and Carmen, for living in a beautiful state of mind.

This book is also dedicated to you, the reader, and to my clients who are a great inspiration to me, constantly expanding my own horizons.

PREFACE

I wish I could throw off the thoughts which poison my happiness.

Frédéric Chopin

Too many of us give up on our dreams when life's problems arise. We postpone our plans until later, temper our ambitions and aspirations, and forget that our future depends on our own actions. We can lose faith in ourselves, and even lose hope. Is this really what we want? This book will help you to identify this type of belief and break the patterns that are holding you back. It will save you time searching for the "right" formula and allow you to test tools and strategies to achieve lasting results in key areas of your life, including personal growth, business, health, finances and personal relationships. You will learn how to take important actions and step out of your comfort zone to allow real growth to happen, and to start living a truly extraordinary life.

This book will support business leaders, executives and anyone who aspires to move in their quest to find harmony and balance in the most important areas of life, guiding them through every step of a transformational journey. Whoever you may be, this book will bring you back to basics and remind you of your vision and goals, so that you can regain control, make informed decisions and build supportive habits to create a life you want to live. It will help you to lay the vital foundations, to understand what life looks like at its best, and to decide your future intentions so that your path is clear, inspiring and full of success. It's your personal life journey. It's a place to plan, visualize, reflect, and prioritize. It's not just about what you get out of accomplishing your goals and achieving success, but also about who you become through this journey. It's about taking little steps at a time, so you can start forming habits that become a way of life, giving each moment the potential to bring you closer to the way you want to live.

I am a coach, mentor and business expert with over 20 years of experience in strategic C-level consulting, human capital management, and art. I have the pleasure of working with managers, leaders, executives, and business owners. My clients come from leading international companies across a wide range of industries, including financial institutions, the pharmaceutical and healthcare sector, technology, logistics and e-commerce, fast-moving consumer goods (FMCG), hospitality, art, media, and the public sector. I gained international experience through projects related to changing mindset, building company success and growth, as well as enhancing operational efficiency and streamlining and designing business processes such as process optimization, corporate performance improvement, and organizational design. I have extensive experience and proven strategies for solving complex problems. I understand the client's position and the environment behind it, and use creativity to overcome any obstacles and barriers. I do not settle for standard solutions; rather, I look for the optimal solution, which may well be challenging for the client. My passion is inspiring people to make big changes, supporting them through this transformation of their life, and continually pushing them to achieve even greater results. Very often, my projects combine both art and business. I believe that the competences and skills used in art may be useful in overcoming recession, creating change and building a stronger, lasting competitive advantage.

Over the last 20 years of working with my clients, I've realized that they do not tend to have the space or tools to explore their full potential to achieve the best possible future. This has led me to write this book, which is intended to act as a roadmap to help you develop your personal strategy and certain useful qualities in the 12 most important areas of your life. Reading this book will enable you to create a growth culture, keeping ahead of change, increasing revenue and optimizing key areas of your business while maintaining the energy and optimism needed to conquer the world. It will allow you to work towards finding clarity, freedom, gratitude, good health, balance, security, intention, authenticity, courage, and joy in life.

Agnieszka
Barcelona, Vila Olimpica, 2021

INTRODUCTION: WHY CHANGING YOUR MINDSET IS IMPORTANT

Most experts and great leaders agree that leaders are made, not born, and that they are made through their own drive for learning and self-improvement.

Carol Dweck

The great many years spent working with my clients have taught me that the right mindset is the key to sustained success. Even the greatest of strategies will not succeed without the right mindset to implement it. When you change your mindset, you are able to transform your life. Most people are held back by their own limiting beliefs, becoming trapped in a cycle of negative self-talk and convinced that they're unworthy or unable of accomplishing their goals.

Capturing the 12 key areas of life, this book will walk you through the different dimensions in which this mindset plays a crucial role. It will encourage you to ask yourself lots of questions that are designed to help you reflect on your current situation and then provoke you to take action, change behaviors and habits, and create better choices to live the life you have always wanted to live – a better life.

All of our perceptions are colored by our mindset, beliefs, values, attitude, personal experiences, emotions, culture, and other factors that create our inner world. We can influence or change our mind about some of these factors and, in so doing, alter our perception of and our approach to work and life. On our way, we might meet lots of obstacles, and our limiting beliefs can distract, worry, and distress us. However, we can learn how to select our thoughts and change the way we act, so that we make better decisions and take a variety of constructive actions. This mental process is focused on changing behaviors to create better results and better performance.

Finding solutions in any area of our life will immediately impact on our personal growth and well-being.

Throughout this book you will observe the use of various different tools and techniques that will encourage you to expand your mindset and bring value and strength to anything you choose to do. It will help you to remove your mental obstacles, broaden your horizons, give you space to think and encourage your commitment to the process.

Mindset is a set of beliefs that shape how we make sense of the world and ourselves. It influences how we think, feel, and behave in any given situation. Our mindset plays a critical role in how we cope with life's challenges. A growth mindset is the belief that people have the ability to develop their talents, abilities, intelligence, and emotional intelligence. It essentially means you believe success comes from the consistent effort to work through challenges. For example, a growth mindset can help you recover from illness because you believe that you can do something about that illness rather than giving up easily. It can help you achieve in sport, in any artistic discipline or at work, and can also help you grow and develop in relationships. On the opposite end, a fixed mindset is the belief that people's basic qualities, such as intelligence and talent, are fixed traits that can't be changed or developed.

A growth mindset helps to navigate and adapt to change and uncertainty. It also enables people to listen, learn, lead, and find effective solutions to challenges. A growth mindset makes people better able to fight back. It also means you believe that you are in control of your own ability, and can learn and improve. Changing mindset is a key element of coaching that I love to work on with my clients as it has such a massive impact on how we behave, think, and grow. According to Stanford psychologist Carol Dweck, when we have a growth mindset, we believe that our intelligence, creative abilities, and character are things that we can improve in meaningful ways. We can always learn and get better at what we do. She asserts that adopting a growth mindset can help us to be more successful and happier, both at work and in our personal lives. Cultivating a growth mindset could be the single most important thing you ever do to help you achieve success.

Each of us has a mixture of fixed and growth mindsets. Although we might have a predominantly growth mindset in one area, there can still be things that trigger a fixed mindset trait in us in another area. People are capable of changing their mindsets and there are some ways to "unfix" a fixed mindset. The following methods created by Carol Dweck, author of *Mindset: The New Psychology of Success*, can be applied:

See the value of the journey. When you're focused only on the end result, you miss out on all the other things you could be learning along the way.

Incorporate "not yet". Even if you sometimes struggle with a task or a new situation, remind yourself that you just haven't mastered it "yet". Once you start to incorporate "yet" into your vocabulary, chances are you can overcome anything.

Replace negative thoughts and negative self-talk with more positive ones to build a growth mindset.

Learn from mistakes. Instead of avoiding the challenges, embrace them.

WHY A GROWTH MINDSET IS NECESSARY FOR SUCCESSFUL LEADERSHIP

Leaders with a growth mindset tend to focus more on the process rather than just the outcome. They know that success comes from the consistent effort to work through challenges. On the opposite side, leaders with a fixed mindset are results-oriented to the extreme. They tend to interpret challenges as failures, believing that all effort has been wasted instead of recognizing the opportunity to learn and grow. Executives who lead their companies with a fixed mindset will create a culture of fear. Whenever problems come up, they will immediately interpret the situation as a failure and look for someone to blame. The leader may even fire or replace the person blamed. This is because they don't believe people can improve their skills to solve the problem. Sometimes you'll also see the leaders stepping in to fix the problem themselves because they don't trust anyone else. As discussed by Daniel Marcos, CEO of the Growth Institute, leaders with a fixed mindset like this can find themselves tangled up in stressful conditions that stifle business growth, such as:

- A culture of fear where their team is too scared to take risks, innovate, or express ideas; they fear being seen as incompetent if they make mistakes.
- An unmotivated team that is not performing at their full potential or expanding their potential.

- Constantly fire-fighting or micro-managing their team, which often leads to people becoming overworked, burnt-out, and stressed.

On the other hand, leaders who adopt a growth mindset create a healthy culture of accountability that drives business growth. Leaders with a growth mindset see opportunities for their teams, even during times of crisis. They don't hide in a corner believing all efforts have been wasted and they don't look for anyone to blame. Instead, they make every effort to accelerate their team's growth to overcome any business challenge. Leading with a growth mindset is critical to developing any team into proactive, accountable, and motivated solution-seekers. And when the team grows and evolves, the company does the same.

Over the last decade, I have studied the critical characteristics of high-performing leaders and their teams, and how much mindset influences resistance to change. I have observed that the old ways of leadership do not fit the world we live in today. Most leaders today are overwhelmed and stressed. They constantly search for different tools and strategies to lead their team more effectively, and to build new habits and behaviors to overcome the crisis in organizations. The global situation has dramatically changed the business landscape recently. As we don't know what is coming in the months or years ahead, in order to thrive, leaders have to master the art of agility and adaptability even more than in the past. For me, leadership today is a humble facilitation of people achieving the best possible results. Any leader nowadays is searching for the answer to the following questions:

- How in pressured times can we manage change and get extraordinary results?

- How in a challenging situation can I help my team to step up and achieve better outcomes?
- How can I shape my mindset to better serve my team and clients?

Exceptional leaders understand that they have to consciously develop their skills and the skills of their team. With strong passion, energy and vision for growth, people will be more willing to follow them. The way they manage their team today requires a new style of leadership that is more focused on facilitation and changing mindset.

APPLYING CHANGING MINDSET PRINCIPLES

Before you start reading this book and reflecting on the 12 areas of inner balance, try to adopt a growth mindset. It will help you to move on in your journey, while a fixed mindset will hinder you. The following is a valuable list of changing mindset principles:

1. CREATE A POSITIVE MINDSET

A mindset is the mental attitude that shapes our actions and thoughts. One of the key aspects of attitudes is how quickly an attitude can change and what implications it can have, as opposed to skills that must be constantly improved to achieve significant changes. This way of thinking is critical if you want to implement changes in your life or the organization you work at. Set a ton of possibilities and channel empathy, integrative thinking, optimism, experimentation, and collaboration. Focus on the good things. Challenging situations and obstacles are a part of life.

2. ACCEPT CHANGE

Instead of fearing or resisting change, make yourself ready to drive meaningful change – whether that means changing yourself, your team, the systems and structures of the organization, or even pivoting its strategic direction and vision. Before you can change and grow, you need to first understand your starting point. What are your own limits, motivations, and emotional states? By embracing self-awareness as an individual or as a leader, you become better equipped to make impactful decisions and explore opportunities to grow in life and in business. It will also help you identify the areas that need more growth for you and your team.

3. INVEST IN PEOPLE AROUND YOU

Create an acceptable environment for open dialogue and transparent communication with the people around you. Set up an agreement outlining how you want to work and cooperate with others. Establish healthy rules. In your professional life, block 90 minutes each week with your team to discuss the most critical issues in your organization.

4. RECOGNIZE AND REWARD THE VALUE OF LEARNING IN FAILURE

Learning to push through failure, treat obstacles as challenges, and persist in spite of difficult situations allows you to lead a team to achieve more impactful goals. Leaders who learn from their mistakes are better equipped to continually push the boundaries of their own growth and that of their teams. It's also key in any organization to create a culture where failure is accepted as a learning tool, as this encourages individuals to grow and take innovative risks.

5. BUILD HEALTHY RELATIONSHIPS

A good relationship requires trust, respect, self-awareness, inclusion, and open communication. Without healthy relationships within your family, friends or team, it's impossible to build a caring and supportive environment. You may check from time to time:

how committed are you? Do you have the courage to raise openly difficult topics? Do you create authentic relationships? Do you support other people? Do you know who is currently struggling and needs help? Do you provide feedback to others?

6. ENCOURAGE COLLABORATION

Look for opportunities with others. How can you collaborate better (even during online meetings) in order to achieve better results? Think about how you can create value by being a team. Coach and develop your team. Encourage interaction and be clear about expectations. Foster honest and open communication. Encourage creativity.

7. BRING ENERGY

There are a lot of frustrations everywhere today. People are tired, losing motivation and the level of energy is lower than ever. Place a high priority on mental health. Think about how far you and your friends, family or team lift each other up. Do you elevate energy by celebrating success and demonstrating gratitude?

8. INSPIRE TRANSFORMATION

As a leader, do you push for innovation and challenge the status quo? Transformation involves working with others to identify obstacles to team cohesion, synergy, and high performance. The leader's role is to turn separate initiatives into a balanced, integrated program of change. As a leader, stress the importance of creativity for the business. Ensure your entire team knows you want to hear their ideas, help them share their thinking, and make time for brainstorming. Empower them to make decisions and take action, and train them in innovation techniques.

9. FOCUS ON THE PROCESS AS AN ONGOING PROJECT

A key part of the growth mindset is to focus on the process and not just the result. No individual, team or company will perform perfectly 100% of the time. There will be moments when results do not meet expectations. This is why it's important to also focus on the process. By focusing on the process, you'll grow yourself and your team to achieve continuous marginal improvements in performance.

Now that you have adopted a growth mindset, leaving behind any fixed mindset that might hinder you, or strengthened your existing growth mindset, you may wish to start your journey by reflecting on and evaluating each of the most important aspects of your life using the free Inner Balance Inventory tool which you can access on my website www.awolinskaskuza.com

HOW TO USE THIS BOOK

The idea behind the Inner Balance Inventory was partly inspired by The Wheel of Life coaching tool. This is one of the most popular visual tools used in coaching to help clients understand how balanced or fulfilled their lives are in six to eight (sometimes more) different areas. For many coaches, the wheel is a useful tool in their coaching practice because it provides an instant overview for both coach and client. The Wheel of Life technique gives clients a helicopter view of how satisfied they are with their life in key predefined categories such as health, finances, and relationships. Sometimes this tool is also used as a self-assessment to become more self-aware and motivated to make changes for a fulfilling life. The original concept of The Wheel of Life is attributed to Paul J. Meyer, a coaching industry pioneer who founded the Success Motivation® Institute in 1960 and built many programs to help people achieve their goals, manage time, and be a better leader. Over time Meyer's programs have been developed. In 2010, successful entrepreneurs Jon and Missy Butcher created a holistic model of questioning everything about how life was meant to work and called it Lifebook. They created an actionable and pragmatic program about designing life into a work of art, with clear goals and progress paths. Inspired by Jon and Missy Butcher's Lifebook, Vishen Lakhiani, founder of premier education platform Mindvalley and author of *The Code of the Extraordinary Mind*, later created his own version and called it the Twelve Areas of Balance. His idea was to develop a system to help people discover the models they should apply to life so that they can consider where they need to upgrade. This approach inspired me to build my own Inner Balance Inventory, which involves the 12 areas that I found to be the most important for my clients during my time working with them. By reading this book you will explore and reflect on 12 dimensions of life. Having a growth mindset is a prerequisite to working through this book, as it will help you to explore the following 12 areas of inner balance more effectively:

1. LIFE VISION

2. COMFORT ZONE

3. CREATIVITY

4. PRODUCTIVITY AND ENERGY

5. RELATIONSHIPS

6. CAREER

7. RESILIENCE AGAINST STRESS

8. HEALTH AND WELL-BEING

9. SPIRITUAL LIFE

10. INTELLECTUAL CAPACITY

11. FINANCIAL FREEDOM

12. QUALITY OF LIFE

Throughout the book, I will encourage you to go through each of the 12 categories and reflect on your answers to some very important questions. Each chapter will start with a set of questions, which aim to make you reflect honestly and without judgement on your current situation. In each chapter you will explore how you can develop in specific areas and which steps, tools and methods you can use. You will then have the chance to decide which you want to select and focus on to find more harmony and balance in your life. You will be encouraged to do some exercises, answer a lot of questions and take actions to apply what you have learned in order to build supportive habits to create the life you want to live.

For most of you, these 12 areas of inner balance are a good starting point. You can set yourself goals and create a new vision for the next year or more. Now, take a moment to honestly evaluate the following questions:

- How do you feel about your life in each sphere?
- What is the most important area for you?
- Which of these areas do you devote the most attention to?
- Which of these areas would you most like to improve?
- What is the value system that governs your decisions regarding status, relationships, financial security, and lifestyle?
- What is within your control and what is not?
- What are your main priorities and what influence do they have over your decisions?
- How could you make space for these changes in your life?
- What change do you want to make first?
- What is a small step you could take to get started?

You need to be clear about these preferences in order to make changes in your life. Circumstances may change, but your underlying values do not. We all know that opportunities will always present themselves, but we can be better prepared for them. In the Afterword at the end of the book, you will have the opportunity to make your own roadmap plan, which you can revisit every year.

Searching for balance and harmony in the most important areas of your life is creative work. It requires effort, consistency, and a lot of energy. Going beyond your comfort zone takes courage and determination, as well as the ability to see your life from a bird's-eye view. This is a kind of mental exercise in which you evaluate your limiting beliefs, fears, and longings, while at the same time looking at where your dreams, aspirations and ambitions come from. By doing this mental exercise, you create a map of yourself and become more aware of where you are now. Frustration in one area of your life may show that in another area something is not working. Very often the changes you want to make don't have to be radical. Sometimes you have to simply experiment and see how things go.

This book is broken down into the 12 steps that will guide you through the process of achieving inner balance. I believe this book will be an inspiration for you to shape, reshape and transform your mindset, and to achieve balance in the 12 most important areas of your life, business, and more. While reading each chapter, you will have lots of possibilities to experiment with the way you think, absorb things, and apply different methods and tools discovered in this book. Are you ready to start?

CHAPTER 1

HONING YOUR LIFE VISION

Forget about trying to compete with someone else. Create your own pathway. Create your own new vision.

Herbie Hancock

INNER BALANCE INVENTORY QUESTION

Before we start our journey and learn how to build our life vision, take a moment to think: how strongly do you feel about pursuing your dreams and goals this year? How vivid is your vision of life?

Write your rating and reflection here. Try not to make judgments, but an honest assessment of how you currently feel.

Rating on a scale of 1 to 10, with 1 being low and 10 being high:

1   2   3   4   5   6   7   8   9   10

Reflection:

In this chapter we will focus on the first area of inner balance: your life vision. You will start to create your roadmap to finding harmony and balance in each of the 12 important dimensions of your life and business. It's a very important beginning to your life journey as it reveals your philosophy of life. It's a place where you will plan, visualise, reflect, and prioritize. In order to do so, you will learn how to create your vision, define your values and lifetime goals, better design your personal strategy, and move forward with the life you really want.

HOW TO BEGIN

Focusing on your life vision is an evolving project. It's never easy, but it's very important to make the right decisions, face the challenges and take risks to live better. Sometimes we know we're not achieving our dreams, but we do not know how to start. Working with my clients, I usually ask: how strongly do you feel you know your true dreams and goals? How vivid is your vision of life?

What you need first is to have a strong desire. You must really discover what you long for. This desire is the starting point because, without passion, nothing can happen. This is a process; this is a journey on which you decide where and when to go. Yet, without specific goals your desire and passion will get you nowhere. A goal gives you a reason, a purpose. Your goal is the direction in which your desire will take you. If you're able to clearly see in your mind's eye what you want, you will achieve it. So, the more detail you see and the more concrete your mental image, the more likely you are to get exactly what you long for.

CREATE A PHYSICAL REPRESENTATION OF YOUR VISION

Before you set your vision, you may want to start by creating a vision board. A vision board (some people call it a vision map) is a visual representation of what you would like your life to look like. You can create one every year and revisit it throughout the year. You may open yourself up to new possibilities and a sense of curiosity about what more you could achieve. You can envision your story for the future. You may want to include pictures, stories, quotes, and words to focus on. This creative exercise can help you get a clear idea of your dreams, intentions and internal motivations in life.

Alternatively, if you prefer not to create a vision board, you may want to create a mental picture of your vision by imagining your life as a long journey and a grand adventure. Put your mind in a place of abundance. Focus on the things that you are grateful to have and the choices you can make. For the next few days write down any dreams you have for your life. Try to be specific and detailed. Use your imagination. Pay attention to which idea keeps coming up, which is the strongest, which makes you feel most scared? Visualization, as well as creativity, can be mastered. They are life skills that can be practiced. When we focus on something with passion, we allow new opportunities to flow into our life. This will give you the confidence, courage and positive energy to live the life you want.

UNEARTH YOUR VALUES

Values help you define who you are and what's really important in your life. What is your purpose? What difference do you want to make? How can you serve others? The values you live by are shaped by many different factors such as your background, upbringing, beliefs, and different life experiences, among others. Values have a significant influence on your behavior and the choices you make every day. Understanding your values brings clarity to every decision you make.

At the top of a blank piece of paper write down five values and prioritize them from one to five. Then spend 10 to 15 minutes briefly defining what each one means to you. Think about what you need to add or remove from your life or what you need to change to live these values. For inspiration, here is a list of values for you to choose from:

- Accountability
- Adaptability
- Affection
- Authenticity
- Balance
- Beauty
- Belonging
- Commitment
- Compassion
- Competitiveness
- Concern for others
- Consistency
- Courage
- Creativity
- Culture
- Curiosity
- Diversity
- Efficiency
- Energy
- Ethics
- Excellence
- Expertise
- Fairness
- Family happiness
- Financial freedom
- Flexibility
- Freedom
- Generosity
- Gratitude
- Growth
- Harmony
- Health
- High performance
- Honesty
- Honor
- Inclusion
- Independence
- Integrity
- Kindness
- Loyalty
- Making a difference
- Openness
- Optimism
- Order
- Safety
- Security
- Self-respect
- Service
- Simplicity
- Spirituality
- Transparency
- Trust
- Wealth
- Well-being

The values should feed into your life vision. If, for example, generosity and concern for others are really important values to you, then they might feed into a vision of your life in which you make more time to help others. A specific goal may be to start the foundation you've always wanted to or dedicate more time to charity work.

DEFINE YOUR GOALS

Goals get your energy running. Goals generate the necessary activity to bring you towards the realization of your dream. A good goal is a statement of what you want, in a positive, clear, concrete way, and with emotion. A goal should be written down, to give it more energy, and should be stated in the present time. You should write down your goal as if you have already achieved it, and start acting as if you are already there. You must be really conscious of the fact you are worthy of having what you desire and you are able to get it – you have everything you need to realize your dream.

Maybe you do not know how to get there right now, but believe in the fact that you will learn step-by-step and be guided on your way by coincidence and synchronicity. Do not limit yourself with self-doubt and self-limiting assumptions. People often quit just before reaching their goals because they lack persistence. You need a positive mindset, consistency, and determination. Take full responsibility and try not to blame others for your problems and past failures. Create your own future.

You will probably know about SMART goals. For example: "By 31st December (put a specific date and year), I will set up a new company specializing in digital transformation services. I will hire a coach to help me do this." Goals must be set in advance and determine your direction accordingly. Goals should be realistic and attainable. The difficulty of a goal is not a deterring factor as long as the goal is practical. Choose goals that are in the realm of what is attainable for you. Goals should be specific and measurable, as well as achievable within a given timetable. Many people spend more time planning a vacation than they do planning their lives. Know your mission and goal-target, plan each stage of your journey before you begin, and your reward will be continual progress and satisfaction. You might want to start with the following steps:

1. YOUR LIFETIME GOALS

At the top of a blank piece of paper write down "lifetime goals". This is your opportunity to think about your future achievements. For example, what would you like to accomplish within your lifetime? This might include moving to a different country, getting married, doing a PhD degree, buying a specific type of house, changing your current profession, starting a new business, etc. There are no rules when it comes to this brainstorming – simply make a list.

2. GOALS FOR JUST NINE MONTHS

At the top of a blank piece of paper write down what you would do if you only had nine months to live. The purpose of this exercise is to help you understand what really matters to you and set priorities accordingly. Often people notice that the things they would do if they only had nine months to live are not on their list of lifetime goals.

3. GOALS FOR THIS YEAR

At the top of a blank piece of paper write down your goals for this year. After completing the first two steps, you will find this step much easier than the others. These are the goals to focus on now.

To help you with this exercise, you may want to ask yourself the following more specific questions:

- If you truly lived your purpose each day, what would give your life more meaning?
- What accomplishment would you be proudest of?
- What kind of job would you like to do?
- What would you do to live a healthier lifestyle and stay fit?
- What would bring more joy to your life?
- What would you like to learn?
- Where do you want to travel?
- How much money do you want to earn/save?
- Where do you want to live?
- With whom do you want to share your life every day?
- Who would you choose to be your mentor?

Ideally, it would be very beneficial to create goals for each of the 12 areas of your life. I encourage you to use the roadmap, which is a working tool to help you make commitments to change and find optimal balance in life. You can find it in the Afterword and return to it as many times as you wish while reading this book.

TAKE ACTION

Most of us know what we need to do, but we don't follow through with the necessary actions to achieve these goals. We tell ourselves we're not smart enough, strong enough, or brave enough. What holds you back is not your capabilities: it's the fear of failure. It's OK to be afraid, but it's not worth letting fear stop you. You may want to ask for help from a life coach. A coach will help you set goals, identify what's holding you back and learn to move past fear. A coach is trained to help you identify those beliefs and break patterns that are preventing you moving forwards. With the help of your coach, you can learn how to take action and commit in times of uncertainty.

MOVE ON WITH YOUR VISION

Keep up momentum and energy during the process. Use these questions created by transformational life coach Tracy Cumming to move on with your vision:

1. WHAT'S YOUR HIGHEST PRIORITY IN LIFE?

Even though it may be difficult, try to answer this question honestly. If you avoid it, your life goals risk being off-purpose. Again, consider what your personal interests are and try to align them with your inner passion and purpose. Your intentions will attract the people and situations necessary to make your dream a reality.

2. IS THIS YOUR VISION, OR SOMEONE ELSE'S?

Make sure that your goals are your own choice, not ones that others think you should aim for. Try to follow your passion and look again at your core values. Focus on the experience you want to have.

3. HOW WILL YOU FEEL WHEN YOU REACH YOUR DREAM?

Reflect for a moment: how will you benefit from achieving your dream? Be specific about the benefits you might receive from attaining your vision. Write down these benefits so they can be your motivators. What exactly would happen if you made a lot of money doing something you are passionate about? How much might your life change or not? Try to be as specific as you can.

4. WHAT STEPS TOWARDS YOUR VISION CAN YOU TAKE TODAY?

Create a support system around you to transfer your intentions into action. Search for every opportunity that is in line with your purpose and vision. Keep the momentum going. No matter how hectic life gets, try to take at least one action a day. Even the smallest actions –jotting down a new idea, reading a single page, or learning one word of a new language – can start to add up. Are there smaller projects leading to your larger dream that can give you pleasure in the meantime? And find a way to measure your progress. Track those little wins by writing in a journal or telling a friend.

FINDING INNER BALANCE

Create your life vision based on your core values. Try to see yourself in the larger context of your life. Look at your aspirations and ambitions. Ask yourself why you aspire to something deeper and more meaningful. Think about what you really want. Consider the many things you want to do with your life and the little time you have each day. Many people spend all their time analyzing, planning, and organizing. Successful people also do these things, but they are very eager to take action. When you take action, things start to happen and become clear.

Think about what you need to change. How does that fit into your lifestyle? Are you comfortable with what you are doing? Are you happy with where you are today? Do you love your job? Do you earn enough money? Would earning more money make you happy? Do you want to start your own business? What really motivates you? Why are you working so hard?

Ensure that obstacles, such as limiting beliefs or negative self-talk, do not hold you back. If you find it difficult to create a personal growth plan on your own, find a mentor who empowers you. You can also work with a personal growth coach who can help you clarify your plan and develop the best strategy to achieve it.

SUMMARY

You have taken the first step and laid the foundations for not only working through the following chapters in the book, but for being a goal-orientated person, powered by your vision, for the rest of your life. You have identified the goals that you want to accomplish, ideally corresponding with all 12 areas of inner balance. You have also had the chance to reflect on what is important to you and what you want to continue doing or change to find more fulfillment and meaning in your life.

Lots of people don't believe they can live their dream. Either they are blocked in some way or they feel they don't deserve their dream. To avoid the pain of feeling they can't have what they want, people often keep their dream so buried that they forget they ever had one. Change is scary. Find a way to move past fear. Everyone has a dream! And you are destined to fulfill your purpose. Why wait?

Once you finish reading the last chapter in this book, you may wish to return to this chapter and revisit your vision of life. I am sure by then you will have greater clarity and the process will be more transparent, so you will be able to reassess your goals and find ways to achieve them. Remember you can keep a note in your roadmap found in the Afterword at the end of the book. Creating a meaningful vision takes time. It does not happen overnight, but if you learn and reflect a little bit every day, you will achieve extraordinary results.

REDO INNER BALANCE INVENTORY QUESTION

In three to six months, perhaps after applying some of the strategies learned in this book, you may wish to go back and reassess the inner balance inventory question. Ask yourself again: how strongly do you feel about pursuing your dreams and goals this year? How vivid is your vision of life?

Write your rating and reflection here. Try not to make judgments, but an honest assessment of how you currently feel.

Rating on a scale of 1 to 10, with 1 being low and 10 being high:

1   2   3   4   5   6   7   8   9   10

Reflection:

CHAPTER 2

REACHING BEYOND YOUR COMFORT ZONE

As you move outside of your comfort zone, what was once the unknown and frightening becomes your new normal.

Robin Sharma

INNER BALANCE INVENTORY QUESTION

Before we discover the benefits of leaving our comfort zone, take a few minutes to reflect: to what extent do you have the courage to do something new, get out of your comfort zone, break patterns that are holding you back, and take action in spite of a fear of failure?

Write your rating and reflection here. Try not to make judgments, but an honest assessment of how far you are currently within your comfort zone.

Rating on a scale of 1 to 10, with 1 being low and 10 being high:

1   2   3   4   5   6   7   8   9   10

Reflection:

In the previous chapter, you worked on creating the foundation for your vision. You worked on discovering your purpose and defining your values. This was the beginning of your journey, during which you focused on creating the roadmap you will later use as you move from one chapter to another. In this chapter, we will focus on the second area of internal balance: your comfort zone. It will stretch you to figure out how to overcome your fears of change, leave your comfort zone and achieve more in your life. This will be a very important step on your journey. You will discover the benefits of breaking the patterns that are holding you back and gain the courage to start something new, or something that you have always wanted to do but previously lacked the courage and motivation.

To make this chapter of practical use, I will encourage you to do an exercise to help you overcome any fear of change and gain the courage to start something new. It's not just a chapter to read, but to really experience something new. This may initially feel uncomfortable but it's ultimately rewarding. So, would you rather stay comfortable or search for your next great opportunity?

DON'T MISS UNTAPPED OPPORTUNITIES

Possibility awaits just outside your comfort zone. In order to change something, you need to change your mindset. Seek ways to alter the way you think and behave, and witness how simple changes can bring satisfying results. In a comfortable, safe work-life schedule – typically a set routine with low levels of anxiety and stress – you may avoid new or different experiences. Such a confining situation renders our abilities stagnant.

The fear of leaving this routine can leave us stuck or frozen. Without a compelling reason to shift gears, escaping our comfort zone remains difficult. However, leaving our comfort zone from time to time creates opportunities to increase our focus, creativity, and drive, and additionally helps us respond to inevitable and unexpected stressful life situations that might arise. In their 1908 research, psychologists Robert Yerkes and John D. Dodson created a model of the relationship between stress and task performance, called the Yerkes–Dodson law, which suggests that in order to increase performance, you must reach a slightly higher than normal level of stress. This "optimal anxiety" exists just outside our comfort zone.

IMPLEMENTING CHANGE EXERCISE:

Do you have a fear of public speaking, networking events, confronting situations, or damaging your reputation by saying the wrong thing?

Rather than avoiding these situations, try to find different ways of acting. For example, if you hate speaking at conferences or interacting during networking events, but feel slightly more comfortable in small groups, look for opportunities to speak with smaller groups of people. In order to step outside your comfort zone, you have to try even if it feels a little uncomfortable, otherwise you will miss out on important opportunities for advancement.

Learning to live outside your comfort zone and deal with novelty, unforeseen events, and uncertainty will make you emotionally stronger and better able to handle adversity when it occurs.

EXPAND YOUR COMFORT ZONE

Change often brings fear and uncertainty. How do you feel in your comfort zone? Are you safe? Secure? Probably, yes: but do you also feel bored, inflexible, and stagnant? Change your mindset and think about how your "comfort zone" is also your "failure zone": nothing has changed, yet you haven't tried anything new either. When you reframe "outside your comfort zone" to mean growth, learning, or purpose, change becomes obtainable. Now think about and plan that next step. Visualize this idea or thought long enough to build solid momentum to take action.

In order to move from your comfort zone to a growth zone, you have to journey through the fear zone and learning zone. The fear zone is when you lack self-confidence, and very often are scared to start something new or unfamiliar. Have the courage to step from the comfort zone into the fear zone. Often a lack of self-confidence, excuses and others' opinions can affect or even deter your aspirations. But once you overcome these obstacles and enter the learning zone, you can gain new skills and deal with challenges and problems beyond your comfort zone.

After this learning period, a growth zone develops. Within the growth zone, you can expand your abilities, realize aspirations, find purpose, set new goals, and aspire to new dreams. Since the process of moving from the comfort zone to a growth zone requires a roadmap and some level of self-awareness, you might experience doubts and frustrations along the way. Sometimes you might even need to retreat back to your comfort zone before gaining the strength to leave and explore the other zones again.

To leave your comfort zone, you need to understand its outer limits and where your panic zone lies. Know that taking on challenges can stretch you, but that these challenges can ultimately lead to growth and learning. Understanding and capitalizing on personal strength proves invaluable. For some, leaving their comfort zone in at least one area of life can bring positive benefits in other areas.

EXERCISE:

Is there anything in your life that you have considered doing but have been too afraid to try? Is it because you are fearful of failure or being left feeling disappointed? Whatever the action is, it will involve shaking up your usual habits and breaking out of your comfort zone.

The best plan of action is to draw up a list of everything that you want to do but consider outside of your comfort zone. You can choose from among the 12 areas of life, but try to be very specific:

- Pick one area of your life you would like to change.
- Think about what new thing you would be willing to do to make it happen.
- Decide on a start date.
- Do it.

Once you take action, you will soon realize that it was not all that bad and that you are far more capable than you imagined yourself to be. Next time, pick another area from your list and do the exercise again. You may find it in your roadmap (in the Afterword). Do it as many times as you need to see the benefits.

Each time you explore the regions beyond your comfort zone, you are growing and learning new things about yourself and the world around you. You automatically expand your life skills and can encourage a sense of compassion, which is a very important quality to possess.

WHAT ARE THE BENEFITS OF LEAVING YOUR COMFORT ZONE?

Dr Oliver Page investigated a number of benefits of leaving your comfort zone (and reflected on them at PositivePsychology.com, where you can also search for other information related to courses, techniques, and tools to help you practice every day). You can see some of them in the list below:

1. OVERCOMING FEAR

Start by identifying the fear that makes something uncomfortable, and then go through a quick mental exercise to rationalize why you shouldn't proceed with this uncomfortable idea. Is it purely emotional or is it a resistance to change? Perhaps you need to proceed and push through any discomfort. It's natural for our minds to resist change. Thinking about taking the first little step activates your brain to take action. Take a goal and break it down into small steps. Focus on one step at a time. This approach will boost your confidence, associating a positive outcome with your goal and motivating you to stick with and pursue it to ultimately achieve the result you desire. You may ask yourself: what's the worst that could happen? And then: what's the best-case scenario? Fear keeps us frozen. These two questions should help you address any fear or discomfort, then channel your energy towards trying or exploring something new. Focus on these positive things and it will be easier to move out of your comfort zone.

2. TAKING RISKS AND INCREASING CONFIDENCE

Implementing something new that makes us uncomfortable can help us build our inner strength and ability to take risks. Even if we fail, we can still learn something new and have an experience we can build on in the future to allow us to lead a more meaningful life. In order to develop confidence, we need to face our fears and take risks. We might be surprised that we are often able to do things we were not sure we could do before. The world is changing rapidly, and those who fear change risk getting left behind. The more goals we set and achieve, the further our confidence will rise.

3. ENHANCING CREATIVITY AND BOOSTING PERFORMANCE

Every job requires problem-solving, especially developing new products, searching for better strategies, preparing for negotiation, creating new business models, and many others. Some difficult, uncomfortable tasks force us to think differently and require us to break down our barriers and our individual limitations. Stepping out of your comfort zone is a great way to boost creativity, and it doesn't necessarily need to be done in front of other people either. You just need to train your brain to think in a variety of different ways and constantly figure out new perspectives. Experiment with new things and initiate new approaches to your everyday tasks. Trying something new will awaken your imagination.

4. DEVELOPING A GROWTH MINDSET

According to the Stanford psychologist Carol Dweck, the growth mindset means recognizing that humans are adaptable. From this viewpoint, setbacks become opportunities for learning and our potential becomes unlimited. Intentionally leaving our comfort zone goes hand in hand with developing a growth mindset. While a fixed mindset keeps us captured by fear of failure, a growth mindset expands the possible. It inspires us to learn, develop, and take some risks, leading to positive outcomes across different areas of life

5. BUILDING BELIEF IN SUCCESS

Leaving your comfort zone means entering a phase of trial and error, during which some level of success is always possible. We tend to be very good at remembering what went wrong but not as great at remembering what we did well. Keep track of your successes and always refer back to them as tangible examples of your capabilities, bravery, and accomplishments. Experiencing this success builds our self-awareness and grows our sense of self-belief.

6. DEVELOPING SELF-FULFILLMENT

For many people, self-fulfillment or, according to Maslow's theory of human motivation, "self-actualization" can act as an important encouragement to leave our comfort zone. According to this theory, in the hierarchy of needs (which operates like a ladder), satisfying our basic and psychological needs is analogous to occupying the comfort zone, while the higher requirements are equivalent to personal growth and fulfillment. This is very important for our self-satisfaction and for expanding our creativity.

7. LEARNING RESILIENCE AND ANTIFRAGILITY

Expanding your comfort zone can equip you to handle change and ambiguity with more poise, leading to resilience. Resilience is the ability to withstand adversity and bounce back from difficult life events. Flexibility, adaptability, and perseverance can help us tap into our resilience by changing certain thoughts and behaviors. Developing resilience is both complex and personal. There isn't a universal formula for becoming more resilient; it involves a combination of inner strengths and outer resources.

In his book *Antifragile: Things that Gain from Disorder*, mathematical statistician Nassim Taleb introduced the concept of antifragility, which is an "increase in capability to thrive as a result of stressors, shocks, volatility, noise, mistakes, faults, attacks, or failures". According to Nassim, although resilient systems bounce back to the same level after a shock, antifragile systems learn to grow from them, embracing new heights. The more time we spend confined within our comfort zone, the scarier new territory will appear to us. For people who are already pushing beyond their comfort zones, change will not seem as frightening. Instead, they'll welcome a new project at work or the opportunity to learn a new language as a challenge that can open up possibilities for growth that were not there before.

Life transitions are all about change. A lot of the anxiety associated with leaving your comfort zone is due to uncomfortable levels of uncertainty. It can make you feel vulnerable, exposed, and fearful of rejection. However, without taking bold action, your life will always stay the same.

FINDING INNER BALANCE

It's worth remembering that getting out of your comfort zone doesn't necessarily have to be a radical move. During my coaching sessions, I push my clients beyond their comfort boundaries to take on bigger risks, so that in the future they don't regret not trying something that they always wanted to do. We build various "what might have been" scenarios. I ask them if there is anything they have always wanted to try, a place they have always wanted to visit, a new project, or a different challenge. I also ask them how they would feel years down the line if they did not do anything about it. Will they regret it? So, I encourage them to do the things that scare them. I challenge them to speak up in that meeting they normally find intimidating. I push them to learn new skills or upgrade the skills they already have. As well as raising their confidence and boosting their performance, this helps them gain new perspectives and broaden their horizons. How far you want to push your boundaries is totally up to you, and will probably differ depending on what else is going on in your life. The trick seems to be maintaining a healthy balance between security and comfort, and a little novelty and excitement now and then.

SUMMARY

In this chapter, you have learned about taking risks and pushing out of your comfort zone in order to explore new opportunities, overcome fears, and deal with change constructively. Stepping out of your comfort zone means you're moving into uncharted territory. You're trying things that you've never tried before, and learning things you've never known before. By exploring the outer reaches of your comfort zone, you will have the opportunity to learn. Every time you take a step forward, you move into a new stage of your life. Try the exercise at the start of this chapter again. Try picking just one thing that's outside of your comfort zone: see how it feels.

REDO INNER BALANCE INVENTORY QUESTION

In three to six months, perhaps after applying some of the strategies learned in this book, you may wish to go back and reassess the inner balance inventory question. Take a few minutes to reflect: to what extent do you have the courage to do something new, get out of your comfort zone, break patterns that are holding you back, and take action in spite of a fear of failure?

Write your rating and reflection here. Try not to make judgments, but an honest assessment of how far within your comfort zone you currently are.

Rating on a scale of 1 to 10, with 1 being low and 10 being high:

1   2   3   4   5   6   7   8   9   10

Reflection:

CHAPTER 3

BOOSTING YOUR CREATIVITY

Imagination is more important than knowledge... To raise new questions, new possibilities, to regard old problems from a new angle, requires creative imagination.

Albert Einstein

INNER BALANCE INVENTORY QUESTION

Before you explore the different dimensions of creativity, take a few moments to reflect: to what extent do you engage in any activities that develop your creativity and stimulate you to proactively change the way you think?

Write your rating and reflection here. Try not to make judgments, but an honest assessment of how creative you are.

Rating on a scale of 1 to 10, with 1 being low and 10 being high:

1   2   3   4   5   6   7   8   9   10

Reflection:

In the previous chapter, you learned about the process of moving from a comfort zone to a growth zone by overcoming fears, taking risks, pushing yourself further, and opening yourself to new opportunities. In this chapter we will focus on the third area of inner balance: how to enhance your creativity in order to hone your critical thinking, develop new ideas, and find solutions to problems. You will find inspiration by using and applying various practices adopted by artistic people to solve problems or think about them in a different way.

CREATIVITY AS A MENTAL PROCESS

Creativity is the mental and social process used to generate ideas, concepts, and associations that lead to the exploitation of new ideas, or, to put it simply, innovation. We are living in an age of tremendous creativity and innovation, and the arts are often at the forefront of such accomplishments. Business and art formulate an intriguing relationship, one that is valuable and tangible. In this unique relationship, art stands as a role model for business and stimulates business leaders to generate breakthrough ideas for innovation, shift perspectives, and build critical thinking and reflective attitudes. Artists, actors, movie producers and directors, architects, orchestra conductors, and many other types of artist can offer different examples of useful media or tools to be used by business leaders. We can find many parallels between artists and business leaders. Both have a guiding vision, possess a powerful point of view, formulate a convincing idea, navigate chaos and the unknown, and finally produce a new creation. Business leaders and artists must be mindful and intelligent in assessing and developing talent. Executives, however, could learn from artists' ability to dare to break patterns, lead changes in taste, and be productive while being frugal.

MERGE BUSINESS WITH ART

There is a pragmatic argument for the growth of business support for the arts: a partnership with the arts provides real value for that business, whether it's based around marketing, brand development, creativity, or staff engagement. However, merging business with art can also generate breakthrough ideas for innovation. Thomas Heatherwick, one of my favorite architects, believes that at the root of everything he does is a fascination with ideas: what ideas are for, what jobs they do. He developed a habit of wondering why things around him weren't better organized: "All I feel we're doing in our projects is trying to make things better." Similarly, I observe while working with my clients that I tend to ask over and over again:

- How can we push the boundaries and improve this process?
- How can we run our projects more thoughtfully – make them better planned, better managed, and better executed?

I understand innovation as a journey. Individuals in innovative organizations learn how to ask questions and actively listen to others. They also learn how to advocate for their vision. They understand that innovation rarely happens unless you have both diversity and conflict. It's a type of collaborative problem-solving, usually among people who have different expertise and different points of view. The same is true for art. Art requires an ongoing search for breakthrough ideas, and the discovery of something completely new by approaching and experiencing the world with curiosity.

According to Marshall McLuhan, author of *Understanding Media*, the power of the arts to anticipate future social and technological developments has long been recognized. Artists possess perceptual abilities that McLuhan calls "integral awareness". Integral awareness first encourages us to think about our practices and ideas. Then it challenges us to step back and examine our thinking by asking probing questions such as: what would you do differently or the same next time? This leads us into exploring critical thinking and how we could create something novel and foster innovation. We will now discuss and reflect on some examples of the attributes of artistic people that are useful to business leaders and aspiring individuals.

THINK CRITICALLY

The ability to think critically is an important skill for any business leader. In today's unpredictable world and state of economic crisis, business leaders have to learn how to make better decisions quickly. Critical thinking is a habit characterized by the comprehensive exploration of issues, ideas, and events before accepting or formulating an opinion or conclusion. Critical thinking skills help with gathering and interpreting information, facilitating effective communication of thoughts and ideas to others, and generating an awareness of our own thinking.

The critical thinking process is very much linked with the creative process. Engaging in the creative process means having the ability to focus on different aspects of a project while integrating numerous tasks simultaneously. According to Daniel Pink, author of *A Whole New Mind: Why Right-Brainers Will Rule the Future*, this also helps develop the right side of the brain. Through the creative process, we can master the skill of questioning, become more independent thinkers, and discover answers on our own. This strategy of essential questioning eventually evolves into a critical thinking process, leading to a habit of constant reflection on work and the ability to give (as well as obtain) constructive feedback.

In projects, I quite often use a tool called the Left Right Brain Matrix to help business leaders assess their strategic ambitions and evaluate where they are today versus where they want to be in the future. They have to discuss future possibilities and limitations in order to decide what support they need and any barriers that need to be overcome. During this exercise, I encourage business leaders to summarize their discussion in the form of drawing. By drawing a picture, scheme or sketch they can create memorable metaphors. It's often difficult for them to start drawing but, once they have actively discussed their ideas, the visual dialogue can help them dig below the surface layer of their perceptions, examine their underlying assumptions, and evoke fresh thinking.

FOSTER INNOVATION

Creating something novel and useful involves moving beyond our comfort zone. Innovation requires integrating ideas to create new and better options. As in any artistic discipline, innovation requires trial and error. What I tend to do in my firm, MasConsulting Art & Business, is to foster innovation through creativity. Usually, I observe whether the environment in the organization is stimulating enough to serve as a source of inspiration.

Do the same and ask yourself:

1. How your office or workspace is designed? Does it embody the idea of removing physical barriers between people to improve communication and promote creative interaction?
2. Are team members encouraged to take risks, rewarded for creative ideas, and not penalized if they fail?
3. Are people enabled to take on assignments that stretch their potential?
4. Do they discuss any foreseeable risks in advance and create the necessary contingency plans?
5. Are they encouraged at all levels to contribute suggestions for improving current business operations?
6. Do you create environments that strike the right balance between the need for improvisation and everyday performance?

7. Do you encourage others to search for different options to solve problems?

What I encourage my clients to do is foster different points of view by seeking outside perspectives. For example, innovation can often spring from reviewing how customers view and use products and services. Soliciting their opinions can provide valuable insight into potential areas for improvement as well as areas which are succeeding – knowledge that is essential for positioning well against competitors. A great tool for inspiration used in design thinking methodology is a "service safari". A service safari requires you to put yourself in the shoes of a user to better understand all the interactions with the service and the customers' behavior. Alternatively, you can go and experience a service run by another business (a competitor) from the point of view of the service user. On this safari, clients become aware of every little interaction that makes up the overall experience. This is a great observational method which allows someone to experience their competitors' services in a real-life environment and reflect on positive and negative aspects.

Creativity is about connecting things. Once we experience something and reflect on it, we can also build on it. When you ask creative people how they did something, it's very often difficult for them to explain initially. It somehow became obvious to them after a while because they were able to connect experiences and synthesize those into something new. The reason they are able to do this is they have had more experiences or thought more about their experiences than other people tend to. The more diverse experiences you have, the better.

During my creative sessions and workshops, I teach business leaders that creativity is not only a talent, but a way of operating. One of the conditions necessary for creativity is an organizational culture that continuously stimulates the development of employees' imaginations. Many of the world's most innovative companies boast a culture that inspires creative thinking. For the last ten years, my company has researched various types of organization, asking whether and in what ways they experiment with using creativity by applying various elements of art to solve business problems. Based on these observations, we have conducted a series of training workshops and programs that help contemporary leaders look for ways to develop their creativity. It has been noted that a small amount of stimulation can instantly change the way people think and look at daily challenges. Based on these analyses, we have created several initiatives and programs that help leaders to unleash creativity, for instance strategic workshops to help manage the process of change in an organization with the use of a symphony orchestra (Management by Orchestra), workshops for leaders focused on thinking outside the box in the style of Leonardo da Vinci and Pablo Picasso, and strategic workshops improving the art of decision-making with the use of stage techniques (you can explore more at www.art.masconsulting.pl).

Many of these programs draw on the mindset of eminent artists, primarily focused on their flexibility and agility. In particular, the way of thinking that guided Leonardo da Vinci and Pablo Picasso in their creative work has been thoroughly investigated. A look at the profiles of these artists and a careful tracing of their approach to work can inspire us to take on challenges. A closer observation of our environment helps us to experiment, take risks, and make new attempts, destroying what is constant and creating new and better solutions. Living at different times, both of these artists nevertheless shared many common features, such as great diligence, above-average productivity (expressed in a large number of artistic works), efficiency, perseverance, experimentation, and the constant invention of new things. They also wrote down their observations, keeping detailed notes and reflections. Both artists are considered to be among the most creative in history.

Drawing on their experiences and translating them into today's way of operating can trigger new layers of energy and unleash a different way of thinking, especially among leaders of interdisciplinary teams set up for specific projects. The key to success here is finding and developing new skills and asking the right questions. The following examples show how, in practice, the seven key skills used by Leonardo da Vinci and Pablo Picasso can be used by contemporary leaders to stimulate and improve creative competences. Below, I re-explore how the principles outlined in Michael Gelb's remarkable book *How to Think Like Leonardo da Vinci: Seven Steps to Genius Every Day* relate to both da Vinci and Picasso, and how they can inspire you to expand your mind.

SEVEN KEY SKILLS USED BY LEONARDO DA VINCI AND PABLO PICASSO THAT GREAT LEADERS SHOULD MASTER

1. CURIOSITA (CURIOSITY)

The ability to ask the right questions allows innovators to survive the status quo and look for new opportunities. Most leaders today who are questioning what to do end up finding an innovative solution as a result of their actions. Be curious, invite philosophy, literature, music and architecture to open the doors to different subjects or sources of inspiration. As architect Frank Gehry said: 'You have to be curious and search out these great works from the past. Not to copy them, but at least to understand what they meant.'

2 DIMONSTRAZIONE (INDEPENDENT THINKING)

Consistent checking of knowledge by building experience, and practicing the art of patience, perseverance, and readiness to learn from mistakes. Searching for sources of knowledge in experience (best practices). The technique of crushing, demolishing (or "deconstruction", a style often used by Pablo Picasso), which involves giving unbridled criticism of already existing solutions. Improving the ability to search for the best solutions by testing, experimenting, learning from mistakes, and drawing conclusions from failures.

This approach is very often used in design thinking methodology, which provides a solution-based approach to problems.

3. SENSAZIONE (REFINE YOUR SENSES)

The ability to improve sensory intelligence, shaping the sensitivity and acuity of the senses, consciously focusing on an image, a desired process, or result. Changing the position of an object is a technique often used by Pablo Picasso and Leonardo da Vinci to change their perspective on a problem and overcome obstacles in thinking. Research shows that the space in which we work has a significant impact on our effectiveness and work atmosphere. Designing a workspace requires factoring in the needs of employees, suppliers and customers. An organizational space that stimulates creative thinking and effective team cooperation fosters more effective relationship building and encourages effective problem-solving.

4. SFUMATO (EMBRACE UNCERTAINTY)

Willingness to accept ambiguity, paradox, and uncertainty. In everyday work, the ability to accept the continuity of change and the uncertainty of tomorrow, and to maintain balance in the face of paradox.

5. ARTE / SCIENZA (ART AND SCIENCE, WHOLE BRAIN THINKING)

The ability to achieve a balance between science and art, logic and imagination. Thinking "with the whole brain", both right and left hemispheres. Developing synergy between *arte* and *scienza* in everyday and professional thinking, planning and problem-solving. Testing the independence of thinking. The use of mind mapping tools as a spatial way of recording information, which favors its processing, remembering, and associating, and stimulates creative thinking.

6 CORPOLITA (MIND-BODY CARE)

The ability to shape quality of life by balancing the body and mind. To stimulate creativity, many organizations create programs that consciously reduce stress and create a foundation for better management of working time. In the current reality, millennials demand greater discipline in the implementation of work-life balance programs (see Steve Fleetwood's article 'Why work-life balance now?' in the *International Journal of Human Resource Management* for more on this subject). For leaders, finding the time for their own reflections and working on themselves and their own transformation becomes the art.

7 CONNESSIONE (INTERCONNECTEDNESS)

The ability to know and understand the bonds between all things and phenomena. Developing creativity through the ability to see relationships and patterns and create unusual combinations and connections. Inductive reasoning by looking for analogies. Deductive reasoning by looking for implications. Associative thinking, aided by questioning, observation, communication, and experimentation, allows you to catalyze creative thought by linking problems and ideas from seemingly unrelated areas.

EXERCISE:

By mastering the seven skills above, you can achieve extraordinary results and find solutions to the different problems you may experience along the way. Allocate time, even an hour per week, to exercising creative thinking about something specific.

One of the best exercises for improving creativity is to practice the skill of presenting a very short and clear description of a new idea. Imagine that you have only 100 seconds to present your idea to others. What will you cover? How will you make it attractive? How will you hold their attention? Write it down and say it out loud.

Like any other skill, the ability to articulate in this way can only come through practice.

FINDING INNER BALANCE

Creativity can be learned and expanded using different methods and tools. You need to find your own ways of mastering creativity by trying different approaches and thinking about problems in a different way than usual. You may change the focus of your thinking, allowing your mind to discover new options. Don't be afraid to try something new. Break free from the limits of traditional, logical thinking and reason. Think more broadly, making every small detail count. Develop new ideas and shape them to fit the situation at hand. Generating ideas is not sufficient; implementing these ideas according to what you need is what it takes to be a success. Use diverse, unrelated data to help you come up with new concepts. Break down data, group them together or even try data you never imagined might work. By experimenting without judgment, unexpected solutions may arise. Sometimes, opportunities are hidden and can only be discovered by thinking "outside the box". Creative thinking is the ability to free your mind to create, interpret, and visualize possibilities.

SUMMARY

In this chapter, you have learned that to develop new ideas or find solutions to a problem, you can successfully adopt various tools and methods borrowed from the art world. The power of art to stimulate creativity and foster innovation lays in discovering something completely new by approaching and experiencing the world with curiosity. You have also explored the seven key skills used by Leonardo da Vinci and Pablo Picasso as great capabilities for you – and any leader – to master. So, what will you create today?

REDO INNER BALANCE INVENTORY QUESTION

In three to six months, perhaps after applying some of the strategies learned in this book, you may wish to go back and reassess the inner balance inventory question. Take a few moments to reflect: to what extent do you engage in any activities that develop your creativity and stimulate you to proactively change the way you think?

Write your rating and reflection here. Try not to make judgments, but an honest assessment of how creative you are.

Rating on a scale of 1 to 10, with 1 being low and 10 being high:

1   2   3   4   5   6   7   8   9   10

Reflection:

CHAPTER 4

MAXIMIZING YOUR PRODUCTIVITY AND ENERGY

The higher your energy level, the more efficient your body. The more efficient your body, the better you feel and the more you will use your talent to produce outstanding results.

Tony Robbins

INNER BALANCE INVENTORY QUESTION

Before we investigate how you can achieve better productivity and energy in whatever you do, take a deep breath and think about your current energy level. How much motivation do you have to take proactive action and overcome your fears and frustrations? How do you build faith and self-confidence? What power do you have to take on new challenges and maintain the discipline needed to act consistently?

Write your rating and reflection here. Try not to make judgments, but an honest assessment of how energetic and productive you currently feel.

Rating on a scale of 1 to 10, with 1 being low and 10 being high:

1   2   3   4   5   6   7   8   9   10

Reflection:

In the last chapter, you discovered how to boost your creativity to foster innovation and solve problems. You learned that you can achieve extraordinary results by adopting certain skills such as curiosity, critical thinking, and using your left brain and right brain. You had the opportunity to find inspiration using and applying various elements of art to find solutions to different problems. In this chapter, we will focus on the fourth area of inner balance: maintaining productivity and high energy. This is a very powerful aspect of your roadmap. You will learn some proven methods to maximize your productivity and produce higher energy, which will in turn lead you to create your own recipe for high energy, productivity, and a successful life.

BEGIN WITH A POSITIVE MINDSET

Do you know that when you're optimistic you view the world around you in a different way, and in different colors? Switching from a negative to a positive mindset enhances your focus and productivity. When something bad happens, do not ignore the negative aspects; rather, focus on the positive sides. You will see more opportunities in life and chances for growth and development. Working with my clients, I observe more than ever that we need power, energy, and a positive attitude to enable us to cope with challenges and remain open to new opportunities and ideas in times of crisis and uncertainty.

Think for a moment:

- What decisions do you currently need to make in your life?
- What are you focusing on day-to-day?
- Do you concentrate on what is missing or on what you have?
- Do you tend to look at the past, present or the future?

Most people constantly concentrate on what is missing. If you do that, you will never achieve high energy, productivity, and vitality. To navigate our way through the natural lows and highs of life, we need tools to maintain our energy and keep us on track. We also need opportunities to get out of our comfort zone, move forward with our passion projects and new challenges, and form good daily routines and habits. We need our own "recipe for high energy" to guide us.

WHAT IS YOUR RECIPE FOR HIGH ENERGY?

Think of it as your toolbox for looking after yourself. You need to identify the things that work specifically for you. Each person will have a different set of tools, which will help to overcome the hard moments in life. These tools will build your daily energy and create a positive environment around you. It could be surrounding yourself with people who are positive, creating healthy relationships or a beneficial work environment, different sports activities, a healthy diet, something for your soul (such as music or books), or visiting places you like.

Your recipe is a kind of go-to toolkit for when you are feeling a bit out of control, stressed or stuck. It's completely within your power to manage your energy levels in a way that works just for you. The human body has basic needs for energy production and maintenance, and addressing them will help you function at your peak.

To stay in balance, your mind needs to be supported just as much as your body. Think about what should be on your daily agenda to maintain an optimal level of well-being. You can achieve this by developing habits that make you feel happy and nurtured. These habits are the key, so ensure your energy recipe toolkit becomes part of your daily and weekly habits. So, go ahead and create your own success energy recipe toolkit today.

ENERGY QUIZ

Try this simple quiz to work out if your energy is drained or you are doing just fine. Your score will tell you whether your tiredness is temporary or longer-term, and how low your energy levels really are.

There are only 18 questions. You can only answer YES or NO. For each YES you will get one point. Add up your score for a mark out of 18.

1. Do you have trouble getting up in the morning?
2. Do you rely on a cup of coffee to get you going?
3. Do you feel tired all the time?
4. Do you often feel foggy, fuzzy, flat, unproductive, uncreative or dull?
5. Do you have trouble concentrating?
6. Do you use sugar, caffeine or a cigarette as a pick-me-up throughout the day?
7. Are you often irritable or angry?
8. Do you forget to hydrate regularly through the day?
9. Do your moods seem to go up and down for no apparent reason?
10. Do you have trouble falling asleep at night?
11. Do you find yourself operating from crisis to crisis?
12. Do you forget to eat regularly?
13. Do you find excuses not to exercise?
14. Do you worry about the future most of the day?
15. Do you forget to have fun, enjoyment, and laughter during the day?
16. Do you fail to have any silent moments during the day?
17. Do you fail to keep a regular night-time routine?
18. Do you fail to have a regular morning routine?

Your score: If you scored between 0 and 5 – You're doing well. You maintain your energy well. You may have difficult moments, bad moods, and occasionally feel tired or distracted, but you probably know how to deal with it.

If you scored between 6 and 10 – You need to take steps to understand what's happening in your body, and how to make better choices to build your energy up.

If you scored more than 10 – It's important for you to create a strategy that works for you to lift your energy levels.

No matter how you score, you can learn how to improve or protect your energy, become more productive, and bring more positive thinking into your life.

PROVEN METHODS TO MAXIMIZE PRODUCTIVITY AND ENERGY

1. CREATE YOUR OWN MORNING AND NIGHT-TIME ROUTINES

You can't produce fantastic outcomes when you are exhausted, so the real key to a great morning routine is a pre-sleep routine. Sleep has a profound effect on our mental and emotional health. It boosts immunity and reduces health risks. So, sleep is important for recovery and preparation. Make sure you're getting at least seven hours a night. If you're having trouble getting to sleep, avoid looking at any electronic devices for at least an hour before bed. Also, keep your bedroom for the sole purpose of sleep. If you want to learn more about sleeping, you can try watching a MasterClass by Matthew Walker, neuroscientist and sleep researcher. He teaches the science of better sleep and explains how sleep affects the ability to learn, solve problems, and harness creativity, and how those skills are affected when you don't get sufficient sleep.

Example of a night-time routine:

- Sleep in a room without any electronic devices.
- Make sure your bedroom is a little cold.
- Do what the Romans did and have a hot bath before you go to sleep.
- Try guided meditations or mindfulness. A regular meditation

practice can help you relax physically and mentally. Mindfulness meditation, in particular, may help improve your ability to release the day's stresses and tensions in preparation for a good night's sleep.
- Listen to calming music. Playing soft music as you prepare for bed can trigger the release of hormones that help improve your mood. Feeling emotionally at peace can help your body feel calmer, too. Try listening to Frédéric Chopin's Nocturnes (e.g., Nocturne Op. 9, No. 2).
- Think about something positive that happened during your day. Every night, ask yourself: what three good things happened today?

It's important to make sure you get your nightly pre-sleep routine right, because this is really good preparation for the perfect morning routine and a simple way to have a productive and successful day.

Example of a morning routine:

- Try to save one hour, or even 30 minutes, in the morning to set yourself up for the day, prepare your mind to think positively, and start your day with power.
- Get up as soon as your alarm goes off in the morning. Do not hit the snooze button. Learn from Mel Robbins' "5-second rule" and practice physically moving within five seconds.
- To achieve high energy every day, apply the 20/20/20 method created by Robin Sharma. Designed to get your body, brain, and mind ready for the day ahead, this method suggests splitting your morning routine into three twenty-minute increments: exercise

for 20 minutes, read for 20 minutes and write in your journal for 20 minutes. (If you feel it's impossible to dedicate a full 60 minutes for yourself in the morning, because you have kids for example, you could try the one method that suits you best).
- Alternatively, meditate to center yourself or do some relaxing exercises.
- Hydrate.
- Write down everything that you need to do and select two to three main priorities. Use Eisenhower's decision matrix tool to help you set your priorities (what is important and urgent, what is important but not urgent, what is not critical but urgent, what is neither urgent nor critical but is causing distractions or are moments of pleasure/fun).
- Prepare a healthy breakfast and listen to some music you like.
- Once you start to work, spend the first 90 minutes concentrating on the single most important project or task that will most benefit your work. Try to avoid distractions during that time.

This will give you some positive energy to start the day no matter how complicated and noisy it might later become. I know how difficult this can be if you have a family, especially with young kids. There will be all sorts of excuses not to give yourself this time. But, try it for one week and see the benefits it can bring you. You might even start with just 15–30 minutes for meditation, yoga, journaling or anything that works for you. Find a morning routine that works on weekends too. Now go back to your roadmap and reflect on what changes you can make to your morning and night-time routines to find more harmony and balance in your life.

2. SEARCH FOR POSITIVE MOMENTS DURING THE DAY

Every human being has more than 60,000 thoughts daily, which indicates how significant the brain's capacity is. A study found that, on average, around 80 per cent of those thoughts are negative. Lots of research on positive psychology confirms that writing down three good things that happen during the day promotes gratitude and will make you feel much better within a few weeks. Doing this fights your mind's negativity bias and forces your brain to look for great things that happen to you during even the most difficult of days.

If you want to feel more energy, ask yourself these three questions:

- Who are the people that fuel my joy and with whom I enjoy spending time?
- Think about ways to bring people who make you smile, lift you up and enhance your mood into your life. Also think of the people who bring your energy down – your energy vampires and hope thieves – and how you can distance yourself from them. Create a plan to spend more time with the people who bring you positive energy. What changes will make this possible?
- What activities make me happy at home or at work?
- A positive nature helps you focus on the constructive things you can learn rather than dwelling on the negative. Name all the positive and negative activities and eliminate those that drain you one by one.
- Which places bring me good energy and inspiration?
- It could be a room in your house; it could be the places you like to visit in your city. We all have places that amplify our joy. Eliminate the places where you do not feel good.

3. APPLY A NEW MODEL OF WORKING TO BE MORE PRODUCTIVE

Try to work in cycles of productive time. Experiment, be creative, and learn each day. Leave your comfort zone (see Chapter 2). Invest in your development. Experiment with 60 or 90 minutes of total focus. Use leadership expert and author of *Personal Mastery Academy*, Robin Sharma's 90/90/1 technique: for the next 90 days, spend the first 90 minutes of your workday focusing on your single most important project. The best results are achieved by doing this first thing in the morning, when your energy and mental focus are at their highest.

Working in 90-minute slots, take a break between tasks. Rest afterwards and allow yourself time for reflection, even if it's just a little rest break to get fully ready for the next session. Don't jump from one Zoom meeting to another. Learn how to use these strategic breaks well. Do whatever will help your brain recover: move your body, eat something healthy, hydrate. The power of positivity can give you the drive to do more in less time.

LIVE BY THESE PRODUCTIVITY RULES

Your productivity can be also increased if you apply the following rules:

1. CREATE A SCHEDULE AND END YOUR WORKDAY AT A SPECIFIC TIME EACH DAY

When it comes to time management, take note of where your time goes. Look at personal data on how you actually spend your time. You can often audit this by using your calendar or applications and accessing a report to find out what's stealing your time. With this information, you can make the appropriate adjustments. Set your priorities and be disciplined about ending your workday at a specific time each day to maintain a healthy work-life balance. Block out time just for yourself: recharge, relax, and do things unrelated to work or home duties.

2. PLAN AHEAD AND GET ORGANIZED

Plan ahead using one of the following options:

The night before: before you leave work for the day, spend the last 10–15 minutes organizing your workspace and creating a list of the three to four most important items for the next day. Learn to prioritize using the Eisenhower decision matrix, also known as the Urgent-Important Matrix. A powerful tool for time management, it helps you decide on and prioritize your tasks based on urgency and importance while sorting out less urgent and less important tasks.

First thing in the morning: during your morning routine, start with the most urgent and important matter from the list you created the night before and work on this when you're feeling most productive. Work until the first task is finished before moving to the next one. Do the most challenging tasks in the morning as this is when you have the most productive energy, you are not drained, and you may have a feeling of accomplishment to get through the rest of the day.

Apply the Pareto principle: follow the 80/20 rule. When it comes to how you manage your time, the Pareto principle can also be applied: 80% of your results come from 20% of your actions.

3. AVOID DISTRACTIONS

Avoid constant distraction and the habit of splitting your attention while working on something important. People tend to balance the needs of messages, emails and to-do lists at the same time as trying to accomplish something, which means everything takes you twice as long. The best way to overcome half-work is by blocking out significant time to focus on one project and eliminating everything else. Set a time limit for each task to prevent you from getting distracted or procrastinating, and remember to have those healthy rest break buffers between tasks and activities.

4. DESIGN YOUR OWN COMFORTABLE SPACE

Try to find a quiet area in your home, free of distractions and separate enough so that you can feel as though you clock off at the end of the day. Be creative. Design your own workspace, even if you do not have a separate room. Use imagination and find some sort of divider to create a distinction between your home and workspace.

Make sure that you have good natural lighting as sunlight can have a direct positive effect on our mental health, productivity, and job satisfaction. You may also want to use plants to decorate your home office, create natural dividers, and uplift your mood. Bringing some beautiful greenery into the workspace will create a natural divider but also will give you a breath of fresh air in your space and help purify the air in your home. The more comfortable and happy you are in your created workspace, the more productive you will be.

FINDING INNER BALANCE

Create your own recipe for high energy and productivity:

- Develop a **night-time routine**: find a quiet moment and ask yourself every night: what three good things happened to me today?
- Create a **morning routine**: apply the 20/20/20 rule created by Robin Sharma and exercise for 20 minutes, read for 20 minutes, and write in your journal for another 20 minutes.
- **Organize your work life** to improve your performance: work in cycles, set up mini-pauses throughout the day between the tasks, rest during your free time, find enjoyment, and work with passion.

By implementing these strategies, you will be able to increase your productivity and maintain a healthy work-life balance. Everything you have read is about taking small steps at a time, so you can start forming habits that become a way of life. Give each moment the potential to take you closer to the way you want to live.

SUMMARY

In this chapter, you have learned how to manage your energy wisely using different techniques. It has helped prepare you to create your own recipe for managing productivity and focusing for a specific amount of time without distractions. You have been inspired by different methods and experimented with the tools created by Robin Sharma, particularly his 90/90/1 rule and 20/20/20 morning routine. The ability to manage your energy is crucial for maximum productivity. Figure out when are you most focused and effective during the day. Look carefully at how and where you spend your time. What do you do for pleasure and what do you do to support your goals? You may want to think about changing the habits or patterns that do not support your productivity. Do not waste your time worrying that you are not achieving your goals. Always measure your progress and celebrate your results. It will help you to gain more energy to finish the tasks.

REDO INNER BALANCE INVENTORY QUESTION

In three to six months, try re-evaluating your current energy level. How much motivation do you have to take proactive action and overcome your own barriers, fears, and frustrations? How do you build faith and self-confidence? What power do you have to take on new challenges and maintain the discipline needed to act consistently?

Write your rating and reflection here. Try not to make judgments, but an honest assessment of how energetic and productive you currently feel.

Rating on a scale of 1 to 10, with 1 being low and 10 being high:

1   2   3   4   5   6   7   8   9   10

Reflection:

CHAPTER 5

NURTURING YOUR RELATIONSHIPS

I am convinced that material things can contribute a lot to making one's life pleasant, but, basically, if you do not have very good friends and relatives who matter to you, life will be really empty and sad and material things cease to be important.

David Rockefeller

INNER BALANCE INVENTORY QUESTION

Before we contemplate how to build relationships, take a deep breath and think about how happy you are with the relationships in your life – your partner, children, parents, siblings, colleagues? To what extent do they offer you support, good energy, and joy?

Write your rating and reflection here. Try not to make judgments, but an honest assessment of your current relationships in general.

Rating on a scale of 1 to 10, with 1 being low and 10 being high:

1   2   3   4   5   6   7   8   9   10

Reflection:

In the previous chapters, after formulating your life vision, you investigated how to reach beyond your comfort zone, boost your creativity, and maximize your productivity and energy using different techniques and tools in order to achieve that life vision. In this chapter, we will focus on the fifth area of inner balance: relationships. This aspect of life influences every other area of inner balance. It's difficult to maintain any relationship, whether professional or personal. People with a growth mindset believe that a good, lasting relationship comes from effort and working through inevitable differences. In this chapter, you will learn different techniques designed to help you master key skills such as communication, commitment, connection, and compassion to nurture better relationships in life.

QUALITY OF RELATIONSHIPS

We all need people – friends, family, colleagues, and others – with whom to share our life, thoughts, and feelings. Even the most successful people will confirm that relationships are crucial to their well-being, confidence, and happiness. According to Marisa Peer, therapist and relationship expert, the key to a successful relationship is "how well we communicate and how effectively we meet the needs of the important people in our lives and how well they meet our needs".

All relationships require effort and attention. The quality of our personal relationships also have an enormous impact on our physical health. Healthy relationships take time to build and need constant work to keep them on track. People in healthy relationships love and support each other. They help each other practically as well as emotionally. They are there for each other in the good times and the bad times.

MAINTAINING HAPPY, HEALTHY RELATIONSHIPS IS HARD

Without understanding relationship skills and how to use them, we may struggle to maintain healthy relationships or know when to leave unhealthy ones. Throughout our life we learn and practice relationship skills such as emotional regulation, conflict management, or empathy, but at an experimental level. We are left to navigate relationships through trial and error, sometimes resulting in toxic relationships that leave us heartbroken or even traumatized.

Following the Pareto principle:

- 80% of your results will come from 20% of your efforts.
- 80% of your happy relationships will come from 20% of your experiences.

This means that if you practice relationships skills – listen more, communicate better, and try to be more understanding – you will reap the rewards of the effort you put in.

Relationship skills are a combination of personal and interpersonal skills that help you elevate the quality of a relationship. They are soft skills that include communication, leadership, and teamwork, as well as emotional intelligence. Just like any skill, they can be developed and improved with time and practice.

Think for a moment:

- Who do you surround yourself with?
- What energy do those people bring to your life?
- In what ways do they support you?

Make sure you surround yourself with people you trust and who encourage you to work towards your goals. Those who are supportive; those who celebrate the important moments in your life, as well as everyday situations, with you; those who believe you will succeed; and those who motivate you to stretch yourself. This might include family members, friends, colleagues from work or other activities outside work, mentors, coaches, personal trainers, groups or communities with similar mindsets, gurus, or role models you know.

Support from family, friends or professionals (coaches, mentors) can increase your sense of self-worth and belonging, give you confidence to try out new things, and help you learn more about yourself. An important question is whether you trust those people. Without trust, you will be left constantly unsure about whether you can count on your partner, family, or friends to come through for you, and whether or not they really mean what they say. Try to connect with people who can inspire you on your journey.

Unfortunately, not all relationships are going to be perfect all the time, but, for the most part, a good relationship makes you feel secure, happy, loved, respected, and free to be yourself. If you are in a relationship that makes you feel fearful, humiliated, or controlled, or in which you are the victim of physical, emotional or sexual abuse, you definitely need to seek immediate help. The end of a relationship can be a very painful time. It may take two or three years for someone whose long-term relationship has ended to recover and put their life together again. Some people develop serious health and emotional problems during this time. Think carefully about who you surround yourself with and any behaviors you do not want to tolerate anymore. You have to decide with whom you spend your precious time, even if you do not yet have the courage to make changes. At the same time, practice and develop some of the skills for better relationships.

THE FOUR CS: SKILLS YOU CAN PRACTICE EVERY DAY TO MAINTAIN BETTER RELATIONSHIPS

Let's start with the four most important skills: communication, commitment, compassion, and connection.

1. COMMUNICATION

Communication is the ability to convey information in a way that is clear, kind, and healthy. It includes non-verbal signals (or body language), which affect the way a message is shared and received. In any relationship, healthy communication encourages us to express what we are experiencing and articulate our needs in an honest and transparent way. It also requires listening with patience and resisting the urge to jump in to fix the problem. People communicate differently, so it's important to work on developing communication skills that best support the individual relationship, even it takes some time to discover what works best. Healthy communication allows you to solve problems and avoid being misunderstood by others.

While communication skills may take time to perfect, here are some great ways suggested by Marisa Peer to get you started:

- Practice effective listening by paying attention to what somebody is saying without interrupting.

- Share your feelings without blame or judgment using "I" statements. For example, instead of saying, "You make me angry," try saying, "I feel angry right now because of this situation."
- State your needs and boundaries clearly and explicitly. Try saying, "Would you mind helping me out with the dishes from time to time?" instead of, "You never help around the house."
- Don't forget that non-verbal communication such as body language is a big component of communication. Be conscious of your facial expressions, eye contact, gestures, tone of voice, and physical distance from someone when talking.
- Try not to get into the bad habit of arguing just for the sake of arguing, choosing not to listen during conflict, giving the other person the silent treatment, or verbally abusing the other person.
- To encourage more open communication in your relationships, set aside time to speak to each other without interruptions.
- Put yourself in the other person's shoes. Rather than being quick to judge someone for their actions, imagine yourself in the situation or circumstances of another person, so as to understand or empathize with their perspective, opinion, or point of view.
- Don't rely on the other person to guess what is going on, or how you are feeling – be clear and explicit.
- Listen to each other, and make sure the other person knows you are listening to them by using active listening cues: keep eye contact, stay focused, do not jump to conclusions, do not judge.
- Let the other person finish what they are saying.
- Talk about things honestly and respectfully.
- Stay calm and try not to attack or be defensive.
- Use statements such as "I feel … about …", "What I need is…"

- Ask for feedback, give feedback, and learn how to receive feedback constructively from others.

2. COMMITMENT

Commitment is the level of dedication you have towards people and situations that are important in your life and at work. It's also the measure of how much energy, dedication, support, effort, and time you are willing to devote to your colleagues, partner, family, and other people in your life and work environment. In a professional environment, employee commitment can be an important instrument for improving the organization's performance and is strongly connected with the style of management. When working with my clients, I often conduct an Employee Opinion Survey to measure the level of commitment in their organization to help the organization find ways to improve the work environment, increase loyalty, and improve performance. You might try doing the same and ask your team:

- Would you recommend your organization to your friends and family?
- Do you agree with the organization's values?
- Do you understand how to contribute to the organization's goals?
- Does your organization inspire you to feel engaged in your projects?
- Do you feel like your progress at work is valued and appreciated?
- Is the level of the responsibility given to you acceptable?
- Are you encouraged to do interesting and challenging work?

Additionally, studies show that commitment is directly linked to the longevity and quality of relationships. Commitment keeps you going when times are difficult. When you are committed to your partner, friend, or colleague at work, you're willing to put in the effort to fix the challenges in your relationship and move forward as a team.

Use the following questions to check whether you show commitment in your relationships:

- Do you keep your promises so that people can trust and depend on you?
- Do you honor your friends, colleagues, and partner, and speak about them kindly, even when they're not around?
- Do you tell your loved ones how important they are to you and let them know they are a priority in your life?

3. COMPASSION

Compassion is an emotional response to another person with an authentic desire to help. It's when you reach out to support somebody you care about while they are going through tough experiences. Compassion requires kindness and being present in the moment. You learn to support in the best way possible based on the person's needs. Sometimes that might mean listening without trying to solve the problem. Compassion at work, or prosocial behavior, is instrumental in coaching. It's particularly helpful during challenging times, or processes of change in organizations (e.g. mergers, restructuring, suspended promotions, or layoffs).

According to Marisa Peer, while most of us do have a compassionate mind, certain conditions (such as stress, feeling overwhelmed, or trauma) can result in us being less than compassionate. Compassion affects our well-being and is essential for social connection. This means that practicing compassion will not only benefit your relationships, but your general well-being as well. Dacher Keltner, author of The Compassionate Instinct, reveals that compassion is something that can be cultivated, because it's not determined by our genes: "Recent neuroscience studies suggest that positive emotions are less heritable—that is, less determined by our DNA—than the negative emotions. The brain structures involved in positive emotions like compassion are more 'plastic'—subject to changes brought about by environmental input."

If you're hoping to strengthen your relationship through compassion, here are a few things you can try:

- Express kindness towards your partner, family, kids, and friends, especially when you greet each other and say goodbye.
- Give your partner, family, kids, and friends the space to feel their emotions. Sometimes, people just need to feel down or upset for a while. Give them time to work through their feelings.
- Listen to them when they are ready to share their experiences and validate their feelings instead of jumping into problem-solving mode.
- Admit when you've made a mistake. This will show them they matter more than you being right does.

4. CONNECTION

Empathy, positivity, and a strong emotional connection drive the happiest and healthiest relationships. Maintaining friendships and connecting with others in a meaningful way help us enjoy better mental and physical health, even speeding up recovery from illness. Social connection is linked to positive emotions and many health benefits including better immune function. Connecting with other people is a great stress reliever, which can also help your long-term health. The best way to harness these benefits is by focusing not on yourself, but on others. Individuals who live a life rich in connections built on compassion, altruism, and greater meaning create a better-quality life.

Here are some ways to build richer connections:

- Be generous and supportive of others.
- Show compassion.
- Show curiosity about people and their lives.
- Show vulnerability.
- Spend time with other people who share your values.
- Propose some kind of valuable solution you can provide.
- Find some sort of common ground.

Meaningful relationships can build self-esteem and make us happy as a result. They can also satisfy higher-level needs such as growth and development. Listening to someone else's point of view allows you to look at life from different perspectives, some of which you may not have thought of before.

FINDING INNER BALANCE

Creating healthy relationships has important effects on the other areas of inner balance, particularly on your quality of life, a meaningful career, and the ability to cope well with stress and emotions. Working on relationships is a lifelong process. Staying connected and developing professional relationships takes time, work, and a tailored strategy. Maintaining regular contact, being empathic, and respecting others also contributes to your own personal growth. It encourages you to think about the relationships within your ecosystem: the surrounding environment, your partner, children, parents, siblings, and friends. A balanced lifestyle means more time for high-quality relationships.

SUMMARY

In this chapter, you had the opportunity to reflect on the quality of the relationships you are building with others. It might hit home how hard it can be to maintain healthy relationships and how many different skills are involved. You evaluated how much support you are getting from the people around you and, conversely, how much they can trust and rely on you. This area of inner balance significantly influences the other areas, since personal relationships at home and work can either inspire you to grow or leave you feeling drained and unhappy. Give a lot of thought to whom you share your time, heart and secrets with.

REDO INNER BALANCE INVENTOR QUESTION

In three to six months, re-evaluate how happy you are with the relationships in your life – your partner, children, parents, siblings, colleagues. To what extent do they offer you support, good energy, and joy?

Write your rating and reflection here. Try not to make judgments, but an honest assessment of your current relationships in general.

Rating on a scale of 1 to 10, with 1 being low and 10 being high:

1   2   3   4   5   6   7   8   9   10

Reflection:

CHAPTER 6

BUILDING A MEANINGFUL CAREER

I've missed more than 9,000 shots in my career. I've lost almost 300 games. Twenty-six times, I've been trusted to take the game-winning shot and missed. I've failed over and over and over again in my life. And that is why I succeed.

Michael Jordan

INNER BALANCE INVENTORY QUESTION

Before we turn to your professional life, take a moment to assess if you are satisfied with your career. Can you say that you love what you do? Do you feel that this is what you want to continue doing? Is your job still a challenge for you? Do you feel passionate about and fulfilled by your professional field?

Write your rating and reflection here. Try not to make judgments, but an honest assessment of how you currently feel about your work.

Rating on a scale of 1 to 10, with 1 being low and 10 being high:

1   2   3   4   5   6   7   8   9   10

Reflection:

In the previous chapter, we concentrated on building relationship skills to achieve more lasting and healthy relationships. In this chapter, we will focus on the sixth area of inner balance: your professional career. You will explore what a meaningful career looks like to you and how this fits in with your broader life vision. You will be inspired to do annual checkups to see if your aspirations, goals and overall professional priorities have changed. You will learn how to navigate your career using different steps and be encouraged to contemplate what a good work-life balance means to you.

A MEANINGFUL CAREER

A career is meaningful when we feel an authentic connection between the work we do and a broader life purpose. To build a meaningful career, you need to first understand what type of work you have an authentic connection to. You have to understand your interests, values, skills, and preferred work style. It means identifying activities that engage you, which you are good at, which give you a sense of satisfaction, and which you can do in a supportive environment.

If you have been questioning whether your current job or career is fulfilling or meaningful enough, that might be a sign that it's time to consider a new direction. Reflect for a moment on what you really want to do. It's important to find support as making changes can be difficult and you may have lots of doubts and fears. This is normal, and support from a coach, mentor or colleague may help you find new perspective. Think carefully about what you really want and what needs to change.

To help clarify these thoughts, try asking yourself the following questions:

- What are my interests? What sort of work am I excited about?
- What are the values that motivate me? How does my career align with these values?
- What skills do I have right now that I can apply to work?
- What is my preferred working style? For example, structured or unstructured; independent or in a team; working with people or working with ideas or things.

YOUR CAREER JOURNEY

Your professional trajectory should be viewed as a long-term project. For this to happen, it's important to gain perspective and understand where you are situated in the market now and where you might be in the future. Advancing in your career can take multiple forms and there are many meaningful choices to make when managing your career. Your career journey can be as unique as you are. Your personal aspirations, hopes and dreams will ultimately be the drivers for accelerating your career progress.

People typically move in one of three directions when orienting their future careers: continuity, change, or entrepreneurship. Career continuity is related to commitment to your current sector: you may be looking for a promotion or to change organization. Consistency and passion for growth may lead you to top positions. However, you may be seeking to disrupt your current career path more significantly by changing sector, function, or even both. Perseverance and resilience will be essential to move towards your goal in this situation. You may also either have already launched a company or be looking at becoming an entrepreneur. You may be part of a growing family business and seeking to innovate from within.

ANNUAL CAREER CHECKUPS / SELF-DIAGNOSIS

Knowing yourself is essential to defining your career aspirations. Once a year it's worth reflecting on how you want your career path to progress and what is important in your current situation and personal life. By doing this kind of checkup you can more consciously decide what you do and don't want to change. A conscious decision made with the support of a coach may help you see more options, and prioritize and balance up your aspirations, desires, and personal life.

Do this short self-assessment to learn how you feel about your current career. Treat it as a starting point for planning your next steps. Answer the following questions:

- Are you satisfied with your career?
- Can you say that you love what you do?
- Do you feel this is what you want to continue doing?
- Is your job still a challenge for you?
- What position do you aspire to?
- What are your professional goals?
- When do you want to meet your goals (1–2 years, 3–5 years, 5–10 years)?
- What are your priorities at this stage?
- Are you heading in the right direction towards success?

- What skills and competencies do you currently have?
- Are these skills helping you or holding you back?
- What new skills do you need to keep growing professionally?
- Is this the right time for training or to focus on a new personal goal?
- How diverse is your network?
- Who among your current personal or professional contacts should form part of your network?
- What new relationship might contribute to your development?
- How do you assess your professional and personal achievements to find happiness and fulfillment, regardless of your age or career stage?

Understanding your strengths and how to develop them, and accepting your limitations and seeking ways to overcome them, are very important things on your career journey. A professional coach can help you set realistic ambitions as you plan your next steps.

NAVIGATE YOUR CAREER WITH SKILL

Everybody needs an internal roadmap in order to have the opportunity to understand their true strengths and aspirations, and look for more meaning at work. As with any journey, there are many possible routes depending on your desired destination and the unexpected detours or paths you take along the way. A career path doesn't always advance in a linear or upward fashion. Changing companies, sectors and roles can all factor in, as well as career breaks.

FLOURISH IN YOUR CAREER

Lay the groundwork for a career that will blossom over time. Sow the seeds of success by developing technical skills and creating quality long-term relationships. Prioritize projects that allow you to grow, learn, and meet people who enrich your own knowledge and understanding. Develop your mental agility and keep innovating by staying curious, trying new things, experimenting, and expanding your horizons. Take care with your personal branding and presence on social media. Share your knowledge, experience, time and dedication with others. Don't approach work in a linear way: take risks, change countries or sectors. Understand changes in the market and the opportunities they can bring.

CRAFT YOUR JOB

Job crafting is the process of adjusting your job description to be more focused on meaningful work. You can start with task crafting. This may include taking on a task that is currently not in your job description in order to expand your skill set, or dropping a particular task from your role to find more time for other things. Another thing is relational crafting, which may be related to the process of purposely creating or deepening relationships at work, taking time to teach new team members, or getting to know colleagues in different departments, building networks, and expanding skills by joining communities of like-minded people. In addition to this, you might consider cognitive crafting. Cognitive crafting is about changing the way you think about your job. Thinking differently about what you do and why it's important can fill your existing role with more meaning. For instance, changing your title to reflect the most meaningful aspects of your role can help you think differently about why your work is important. Being involved in a completely different project can change the way you think about your current role too. Whatever you consider or would apply to craft your job, improving any area will help you to feel more satisfied in your job and may lead you to further changes in your current role. If you are interested in learning more about job crafting, see Madelyn Geldenhuys' article 'How task, relational and cognitive crafting relate to job performance: a weekly diary study on the role of meaningfulness' in the *European Journal of Work and Organizational Psychology*.

GET UNSTUCK

Start by auditing your current job. What changes can you make to the work you do or the relationships you're building? Minor modifications to how you approach each day can have a major impact on how you feel about the work you're doing. Remember you are in charge of your life and your career. You know what is important to you. With the right help from a career coach, you can define your career ambitions and look at the steps needed to make your career goals happen, including actively looking for ways to improve your job skills or make a big change.

TRANSITION TO A CAREER THAT MAKES YOU EXCITED TO GO TO WORK EVERY DAY

DEVELOP YOUR PASSION

Without heart and drive, you'll never reach your full potential. Rather than choosing a job for the money, choose it for your own personal growth, satisfaction and happiness. Ask yourself: do you do what you love? What can you offer that is unique? Try to build your vision from there. Secure your finances. Sometimes, you will have to sacrifice your resources to do what you love. In reality, pursuing your passions will not guarantee a great salary immediately. So, don't just impulsively quit your job to chase your dreams. Be intentional in studying your passion before you jump into pursuing it full-time. Always take calculated risks.

Find a mentor or career coach You may already know that you want a career change but not know where to start. If you feel suffocated in your current job, then a career coach will be able to help you. A career coach provides unbiased, objective feedback tailored to your search and career goals. A professional coach of this type will get to know your skills and aptitudes and then help you achieve your goals. In any career, mentorship is of utmost importance. A coach or mentor will guide your next steps with greater insight and perspective. You will have a clearer view of what you should and should not do.

EXPLORE THE POSSIBILITIES

Think about what you really want and what needs to change. Maybe your values no longer align with those of your company. Or perhaps you long for a job that offers the ability to travel internationally. Spend some time understanding what is making feel you unsatisfied, even if you don't yet know what to do about it. Once you have a clear idea of your dream job, it's time to start exploring. Open yourself up to the possibilities. Tap into your network. Leverage platforms like LinkedIn to find people in the profession you'd like to pursue. Find out how they got to where they are. What does a day in the life of this person look like? Is it what you envisioned, or does the reality seem different? Can you identify any gaps you would need to fill to achieve your goals, such as additional skills, training, and qualifications?

Consider other ways to research different careers such as books, podcasts, virtual conferences, and professional associations. Concentrate on what you are naturally talented at so you can go from good to great. People who use their strengths at work are more energetic, confident, healthy, creative, satisfied, and engaged. Start applying for roles that are in line with your vision.

BUILD YOUR UNIQUE BRAND

Your personal brand is at the center of who you are and how others see you. You need to spend some time thinking about how to convincingly communicate your unique value proposition and whether the story you tell is memorable enough. Start with optimizing your profile on LinkedIn and making impactful connections. You will gain greater visibility once you begin to publish on LinkedIn.

NETWORK

Building a strong network is essential to unlocking the "hidden" job market. Gain real-life insights and advice through using different tools that connect you with other professionals and nourish a long-lasting career network. Talk to key people to generate opportunities.

WHAT DOES A WORK-LIFE BALANCE MEAN TO YOU?

For most people, a work-life balance does not exist. Others perceive it as making a bigger impact at work and in the world without sacrificing personal health or happiness. It's about prioritizing what's important, including self-care without guilt, shame or apology, having strong boundaries and letting go of trying to do, and have, it all. This means that work-life balance is really about feeling content with who you are and the decisions you make. It begins with your mindset. And it's not something that you find. You create the balance through making tough choices.

To establish a work-life balance, you'll need to:

- Prioritize what's truly important to you.
- Take control over your career path.
- Simplify your life.

All of these require courage, mental strength, and resilience as they are not easy things to do. In order to make these tough choices, you'll want clarity around why. That's also what's causing much of your stress. By agreeing to take on more work than you have capacity for or failing to delegate work that could be delegated, you're creating more stress for yourself. But you can always say no to things that aren't priorities, delegate as much as possible, and really prioritize your own well-being. Making tough choices requires you to create strong boundaries, even at work. Saying no kindly (without guilt) is a skill that can be developed. One of the biggest reasons work-life balance is important relates to your mental health. When you feel balanced, you're more capable of dealing with negative emotions and thoughts. The human brain isn't meant to feel stressed-out and under pressure all the time. When you're stressed, overwhelmed or anxious, you lose the capacity to think creatively. But with balance comes clear, creative thinking. And that means a better work product too.

FINDING INNER BALANCE

To get where you want to go, you need a plan. A career plan is a very valuable instrument that allows you to take the pulse of your career, evaluate where you're at presently and, above all, consider what you can and want to become in the future. Think about what you really want or what is right for you: is it a promotion, a lateral move, or new challenges outside your current company? Doing a career-planning evaluation from time to time is important to assess your professional direction and achieve a work-life balance.

SUMMARY

In this chapter, you have reflected on what your career really means to you. We've covered how important it is to do an annual self-diagnosis, checking in on your priorities and updating your career plan if needed. You have uncovered that achieving your ideal work-life balance involves making tough choices, which can also impact on aspects of your life outside of your work. Exploring possibilities and being open to new opportunities can transform your career into an open book with blank pages ready for you to write. With an open mind you can achieve more than you ever expected.

REDO INNER BALANCE INVENTORY QUESTION

In three to six months, re-evaluate whether you are satisfied with your career. Can you say that you love what you do? Do you feel that this is what you want to continue doing? Is your job still a challenge for you? Do you feel passionate about and fulfilled by your professional field?

Write your rating and reflection here. Try not to make judgments, but an honest assessment of how you currently feel about your work.

Rating on a scale of 1 to 10, with 1 being low and 10 being high:

1 2 3 4 5 6 7 8 9 10

Reflection:

CHAPTER 7

BECOMING MORE RESILIENT AGAINST STRESS

If your emotional abilities aren't in hand, if you don't have self-awareness, if you are not able to manage your distressing emotions, if you can't have empathy and have effective relationships, then no matter how smart you are, you are not going to get very far.

Daniel Goleman

INNER BALANCE INVENTORY QUESTION

Before we learn about how to become more resilient, change our outlook on stress and cope with our emotions, take stock of how you currently deal with stress, anxiety, panic, fear, emotional overload, and doubts. Is there too much stress in your life? To what extent can you shift your attitude towards finding solutions rather than being bothered by the problems?

Write your rating and reflection here. Try not to make judgments, but an honest assessment of how you currently cope.

Rating on a scale of 1 to 10, with 1 being low and 10 being high:

1   2   3   4   5   6   7   8   9   10

Reflection:

In the previous chapter, we reflected on building a meaningful career, which involved looking at how we deal with certain situations related to our career and professional choices and using opportunities to move our career path in the direction we want. In this chapter, we will focus on the seventh area of inner balance: becoming more resilient against stress. Beyond the applications of therapy or coaching, reframing and resilience are also highly useful tools in the workplace. In this chapter, you will be guided through how to reframe stressful situations. You will have the chance to practice a valuable three-step exercise to learn how to cope with everyday stress and emotions.

REFRAME CHALLENGING SITUATIONS

Like instruments, we are very fragile and sensitive to the changes in our environment, even our internal environment. Often, we are disappointed to see that the world is not how we expected. However, we humans have the ability to reframe any situation that confronts us. Reframing is a technique used to shift our mindset so that we can see situations from another, usually more positive, perspective. It can be tremendously helpful in problem-solving, decision-making, and learning. Reframing helps you move on from a situation in which you feel stuck or confused more constructively. Leaders can use reframing to resolve employee conflict, enhance problem-solving, or even reduce feelings of burnout or being overwhelmed.

The essential idea behind reframing is that the frame through which a person views a situation determines their point of view. Reframing is a conscious activity that requires will and effort. However, after time it can become a habit which essentially results in a change in mindset about how situations are perceived. Positive reframing involves thinking about a negative or challenging situation in a more positive way. This could involve thinking about a benefit or upside to a negative situation that you had not previously considered.

HOW TO REFRAME YOUR THOUGHTS

Step 1: Identify the problem.

>Identify the problem, state or limiting behaviour that you are having difficulty with.

Step 2: Write down the situation or problem.

>Try to be specific and honest with yourself.

Step 3: Challenge your assumptions.

>Write down your thoughts, feelings, and emotions about the situation.

Step 4: Reframe your circumstances.

>Create a few alternative thoughts. List evidence to support these alternative thoughts.

Step 5: Test the reframe.

>See if it's more comfortable and less stressful. Can you more easily accept it? Does the reframe pass the test, so to speak?

HOW TO PRACTICE REFRAMING

Reframing can be a highly effective leadership tool. You can explore stressful or difficult situations by asking the following reframing questions:

- How accurate is your interpretation of the situation?
- What other things might be going on (e.g. other factors or problems)?
- Is there a different way to view this?
- How might someone else perceive this?

The point is to open up a dialogue in respect of all the different possibilities surrounding a situation, not to decide which interpretation is correct. This allows us to see things from a different perspective, which can help reduce stress and improve problem-solving. When your stress reaction isn't triggered, you are able to see all the options more clearly and make decisions based on logic, rather than purely on emotion. In my coaching practice, I have observed that often when people have difficulty making a decision or imagining a solution, it isn't because they don't understand the process of problem-solving; it's because they are stuck in their perception of the situation. Usually, they can only see limited possibilities. Reframing allows them to discover a variety of different options and outcomes.

STRESS IS INEVITABLE AND HAS MANY SOURCES

Although you have learned how to experiment with reframing and resolving a problem by looking at it in a new way, stress is still an inevitable part of life. The word 'stress' is used to describe a wide range of feelings, symptoms, and situations. These feelings are almost always linked or associated with situations at work and home which involve:

- Being under lots of pressure.
- Facing big or frequent changes.
- Quality of working relationships.
- Worrying about something (money, long-term unemployment, retiring, starting a new job).
- Health problems.
- Traumatic events.
- Not having much or any control over the outcome of a situation.
- Having overwhelming responsibilities.
- Times of uncertainty.

Stress is a reality, and it's not possible to lead a completely stress-free life. Therefore, people need to be aware of its existence and learn to live with it without suffering its ill effects. As reported by Tracy Herbert and Sheldon Cohen (Carnegie Mellon University) in their article 'Depression and immunity: A meta-analytic review' in *Psychological Bulletin*, people's responses to stress vary widely depending on their cultural and family backgrounds, personal experiences, mood, and other stresses that might be affecting them at the same time. However, when problems escalate faster than they can be solved, a person's adaptive capacity may be overloaded and chronic illness, anxiety or depression may result.

NEGATIVES OF STRESS

In the report 'Psychological Stress and the Human Immune System: A Meta-Analytic Study of 30 Years of Inquiry' in *Psychological Bulletin*, developed by Suzanne Segerstrom (University of Kentucky) and Gregory Miller (University of British Columbia) to describe the relationship between psychological stress and the immune system in human participants, we learn that prolonged stress can result in suppressed immune function and an increased tendency to have infectious and immune-related diseases. Emotional stress can also result in hormonal imbalances that further interfere with healthy immune functioning. Stress also affects mental fitness, memory, and learning capabilities. There are many different causes of stress, and each person processes and responds to their stressors differently. Stress affects our mood and can be expressed in the form of irritability, mood swings, depression, and sadness. It can lead us to focus on the negative, feel overwhelmed, and experience anxiety. At work this can lead to a lack of motivation and concentration, increased conflicts between individuals, reduction in performance, high levels of sickness and absenteeism, a lower level of productivity, and failure to meet targets.

OUR THOUGHT PROCESSES INVITE STRESS

Although we hear a lot about the negative side of stress, interestingly there are some positive effects of stress too. According to researchers Daniel Kaufer and Elizabeth Kirby from the University of California, Berkeley, moderate stress strengthens the connection between neurons in our brain, improving memory and attention span, and helping us become more productive. "I think intermittent stressful events are probably what keeps the brain more alert, and you perform better when you are alert," posited Professor Kirby. Stress may enhance motivation. For example, the stress of a tight deadline can help people focus because time is running out. We have all experienced a time when we struggled to start preparing for something (e.g. an exam, project or new task) and procrastinated until the last moment, unable to find the motivation to work on it until we reached that state of stress.

In some situations, stress encourages growth. Even though stress may feel overwhelming, it also forces people to problem-solve, ultimately building confidence and skills that are important for future experiences. It's not easy, but with increased resiliency and confidence, people tend to feel less threatened and more in control of their situation. It can also help us work through experiences instead of avoiding them. After facing a fear, we may feel more equipped to handle it in the future. With so much stress every day, it's necessary to learn how to recover quickly from difficulties, overcome hardship and work through problems, and return to normal life stronger than we were before.

WHAT IS RESILIENCE?

Psychologists define resilience as the process of adapting well in the face of adversity, trauma, tragedy, threats, or significant sources of stress, such as family and relationship problems, serious health problems, or workplace and financial stressors. As much as resilience involves "bouncing back" from these difficult experiences, it can also involve profound personal growth. While these adverse events are certainly painful and difficult, they don't have to determine the course of your life. There are many aspects of your life you can control and modify. That's the role of resilience. Becoming more resilient not only helps you get through difficult circumstances, it also empowers you to grow and even improve your life along the way.

While resilience is when you can bounce back from adversity, according to Dr Srikumar Rao, speaker, author, former business school professor and creator of the Creativity and Personal Mastery program, "extreme resilience is the ability to do that very quickly – to bounce back from any challenge, problem or setback so quickly that your journey isn't impacted at all."

We know that stress will always appear (e.g. relationship problems, illness, financial setbacks, business issues). Stress can be described as a natural byproduct of believing that your reality should somehow be other than it currently is. When this happens, you have two choices:

1. No matter what happens, find a way to deal with it.
2. Give up.

So, what creates the need to bounce back in the first place? Is it "adversity" or is it something else? According to Dr Rao, the feeling you have when you get "knocked down" and have to bounce back is a byproduct of the mental models through which you filter the events of your life. Mental models are your rules about how life is supposed to go and what it means if it doesn't quite go that way.

APPLY THE FOUR CORE COMPONENTS OF RESILIENCE

Resilience involves behaviors, thoughts, and actions that anyone can learn and develop. Increasing your resilience takes time and purpose. You can start by focusing on four core components: connection with others, wellness, healthy thinking, and meaning.

Try to apply the following guidelines to practice your skills:

1. Connect with others

Connecting with empathetic and understanding people can remind you that you're not alone in the midst of difficulties. Focus on finding trustworthy and compassionate individuals who validate your feelings. The pain of traumatic events can lead some people to isolate themselves, but it's important to accept help and support from those who care about you. Try to prioritize genuinely connecting with people who are around you and understand you.

2. Take care of your body

Self-care may be a popular buzzword, but it's also a legitimate practice for mental health and building resilience. That's because stress is just as much physical as it is emotional. Promoting positive lifestyle factors like proper nutrition, sleep habits, hydration, and regular exercise can strengthen your body to adapt to stress and reduce anxiety or depression.

3. Practice mindfulness

Mindful journaling, yoga, and other practices like meditation can also help people build connections and restore hope, which helps prime them to deal with situations that require resilience. When you journal, meditate, or pray, reflect on positive aspects of your life and recall the things you're grateful for, even during personal trials.

4. Avoid negative outlets

It may be tempting to mask your pain with alcohol, drugs, or other substances, but that does not solve the problem. Focus instead on giving your body resources to manage stress, rather than seeking to eliminate the feeling of stress altogether.

RESTORING EMOTIONAL EQUILIBRIUM

Change is stressful because it requires us to adapt and transform our way of thinking. Experiencing too many changes within a brief time period often makes us feel as though we aren't in control of events. This perception contributes to low self-esteem and may even lead to the onset of anxiety or depression. In some cases, physical illnesses may develop or get worse when a person's capacity to adapt is overwhelmed by too much change. It's important to learn how to cope with stress and emotions. It involves adjusting to or tolerating negative events or realities while you try to maintain a positive self-image and emotional equilibrium. Coping occurs in the context of life changes that are perceived to be stressful and usually associated with negative life changes, such as losing a job or loved one. However, all change requires some sort of adaptation. Even positive changes such as getting a promotion, going on vacation, getting married or having a child can generate stress. Coping involves adjusting to unusual demands or stressors. This requires making a greater effort and using more energy than needed in the daily routines of life.

DO THIS THREE-STEP EXERCISE IN HOW TO COPE WITH STRESS AND EMOTIONS

Try practicing this exercise designed by Dr Rao any time during the day or last thing in the evening. The benefit of doing this exercise will be learning how to change your thinking about stress.

Step 1: Get in the habit of being grateful

According to Dr Rao, the first step in the exercise is to be grateful: not grateful for something in particular, just grateful. This helps to develop the habit of detaching gratitude from outcomes. It's easy to be grateful when things are going the way you want, but being grateful because you choose to be is much more powerful. It's important to remember that gratitude is not a thought, it's a feeling that you can practice by drawing on a time in your past when you truly did feel grateful. As Dr Rao recommends: "Bring that memory to the present in the form of feeling and practice recalling that into your body as quickly as you can. What might gratitude feel like? It may feel like wholeness. It may feel like the absence of need. It may also feel like a joyful, but quiet, peace."

Step 2: Quiet your mental chatter

The voice inside your mind, your mental chatter, is a byproduct of your current mental models and it does not create the events in your life. Rather, it creates the stories you tell yourself about the events in your life in your own words. "This is good, that is bad, I want this to happen, I don't want that to happen." The art of learning to quiet this chatter helps to create the space required to choose how you will respond to what happens to you in your life. One effective strategy to quiet your mental chatter is to locate your awareness on your breathing. You may try different breathing techniques for stress relief, or to reduce anxiety and find what works for you, or simply close your eyes and focus on your breathing. Dr Rao reminds us that "if you're feeling something other than what you want to feel, you are using a mental model that does not serve you. The challenge is to stop believing your mental model about the way you think the world works. Every problem in our life, including stress, is something we create by believing that reality should be, in some way, other than it actually is."

Step 3: Exercise your power to choose

Remember that, in all situations, you have the power to choose the emotional domain you occupy and the way you experience life events. You have the power to choose the story you tell yourself, or whether you tell yourself a story at all. You may wish to practice Dr Rao's mental model called 'Wonderful, No Matter What', or if you prefer, you can also call it by its other name: 'Is It Good? Is It Bad? Who Knows?' By applying this model, you occupy the emotional domain where events are received with gratitude and an understanding that they all play a part in your own unique journey. It's not about ignoring reality but looking at life through a lens that serves you instead of disturbs you. This will help you "bounce back" instantly from any challenge, mainly because you no longer have a mental model that interprets the events of life as something to "bounce back" from.

As you repeat this practice you will begin to notice that "stress" as you used to know it stops making such frequent appearances in your life. Eventually, you will prove to yourself that the "stress" you used to experience was actually something you created.

Change affects people differently, bringing a unique flood of thoughts, strong emotions, and uncertainty. People generally adapt well over time to life-changing situations and stressful situations thanks in part to resilience.

FINDING INNER BALANCE

People differ in their particular styles of coping with stress and emotions, and prefer to use certain strategies over others. These differences in coping style usually reflect differences in personality. It's especially important to evaluate your lifestyle when encountering significant stress. Engaging in stress-reducing activities may help your overall approach to dealing with stressors. In particular, practicing resilience-building skills will offer you the opportunity to persevere and continue to function effectively despite failures, setbacks, and losses.

Here are some different coping strategies that you may wish to apply:

- Get enough good quality sleep.
- Eat a well-balanced diet.
- Exercise on a regular basis.
- Take brief rest periods during the day to relax.
- Take vacations away from home and work.
- Engage in pleasurable or fun activities every day.
- Practice relaxation exercises such as yoga, prayer, meditation, or progressive muscle relaxation.
- Avoid caffeine and alcohol.
- Adjust your expectations.
- Ask others to help or assist you.

SUMMARY

In this chapter, you have learned how to cope with stress and emotions by reframing and developing resilience. Reframing may challenge your existing interpretations in order to see what other possibilities exist, and can help you transform a stressful situation into one that's a bit easier to overcome. Resilience, on the other hand, helps you withstand adversity and bounce back from difficult life events.

REDO INNER BALANCE INVENTORY QUESTION

In three to six months, perhaps having applied some of the strategies learned in this chapter, go back and reassess the inner balance inventory question. How do you deal with stress, anxiety, panic, fear, emotional overload, and doubts? Is there too much stress in your life? To what extent have you changed your attitude towards finding solutions rather than being bothered by the problems?

Write your rating and reflection here. Try not to make judgments but just an honest assessment of how you currently cope.

Rating on a scale of 1 to 10, with 1 being low and 10 being high:

1   2   3   4   5   6   7   8   9   10

Reflection:

CHAPTER 8

TAKING CONTROL OF YOUR HEALTH AND WELL-BEING

If we could give every individual the right amount of nourishment and exercise, not too little and not too much, we would have found the safest way to health.

Hippocrates

INNER BALANCE INVENTORY QUESTION

Before we dig deeper into examining health and fitness, take a deep breath and rate your health, mental condition, fitness, appearance, dietary habits, immune system, sleep quality, and concentration. What is your level of taking control of health and well-being?

Write your rating and reflection here. Try not to make judgments, but an honest assessment of your health and well-being.

Rating on a scale of 1 to 10, with 1 being low and 10 being high:

1   2   3   4   5   6   7   8   9   10

Reflection:

In the previous chapter, we explored how to cope with stress and emotions by applying different components of resilience skill-making and reframing strategies. In this chapter, we will focus on the eighth area of inner balance: healthy habits to encourage mental stability and activities that affect your physical condition, energy, and lifestyle. You will also discover the concept of longevity, which will inspire you to implement strategies to improve your chances of living a longer and healthier life.

MAINTAINING GOOD HEALTH

Being healthy and fit allows you to stay active and increases your confidence and concentration power. Maintaining good health doesn't happen by accident. It requires work, smart lifestyle choices, and the occasional checkup and test. Healthy habits improve your physical appearance, mental stability, and ability to perform activities. In turn, this helps you lead a stress-free lifestyle and maintain happier moods and high energy levels.

Health can generally be measured according to three major parameters:

- Physical
- Nutritional
- Psychological

Physical health denotes a person's physical appearance, cardiovascular fitness, stamina, strength, flexibility, and mobility. Nutritional health means the presence of essential nutrients in the body needed to grow, regenerate, have high energy levels, and fight disease. Psychological health signifies a person's ability to maintain patience, calm, and composure in all circumstances of life as well as resilience, emotional intelligence, a positive outlook, and ability to cope with life's stresses.

A person who is both physically and mentally fit is strong enough to face the ups and downs of life. They have a higher chance of living life to the fullest, without major medical or physical issues. However, it's also worth establishing a good relationship with a primary care physician or a holistic doctor. Somebody who will recommend that you test to check for hidden disease at least once a year. Having a healthy lifestyle leads to happiness, success, and achievement. Being happy is directly related to boosting your mental strength and health, so happiness can be considered a result of, as well as part of, a healthy and fit lifestyle.

HOW TO DEVELOP GOOD HABITS

Health is the single most important thing you should take care of. By developing good habits, you make your health a priority. You should create a plan to ensure you make the effort to maintain your physical and mental well-being every single day. Use the three simple strategies developed by James Clear, author of Atomic Habits, to create long-lasting habits, get motivated to work out, and turn exercise into a routine:

1. Develop a ritual to make starting easier and create an implementation intention.

For example, you could set your intention to exercise by filling out this sentence: Next week, I will exercise on [DAY] at [TIME OF DAY] at/in [PLACE].

2. Start with an exercise that is so easy that you can do it even when your energy is very low.

Focus on finding a way to get started in less than two minutes rather than worrying about your entire workout. Simply fill up your water bottle and put on your running shoes.

3. Focus on the habit first and the results later.

In the first six months, it's more important not to miss workouts than it is to make progress. Set a time limit for the task and concentrate on doing it regularly (e.g. 20 minutes of running, or 15 minutes of yoga).

Once you have built the habit of exercise, you can find thousands of ways to improve. Without the habit, every other strategy is useless.

BE PHYSICALLY ACTIVE

Physical activity is very important for good health. According to Professor Darren Warburton from the University of British Columbia and author of the review 'Health benefits of physical activity: the evidence', physical activity can greatly reduce the risk of heart disease, stroke, diabetes, breast and colon cancer, depression, and falls. Physical activity improves sleep, endurance, and even sex. You may enjoy spending time outdoors in the sun inhaling fresh air and taking part in healthy activities such as:

- Walking
- Running
- Cycling
- Swimming
- Gardening
- Skipping
- Yoga

It's recommended to aim for 90 minutes of moderate-intensity exercise, such as brisk walking, every week together with strength training, which is important for balance, bone health, controlling blood sugar, and mobility, two to three times per week.

Natural changes to the body as we age can lead to a gradual loss of muscle, reduced energy, and achy joints. These changes may make it tempting to move less and sit more. But doing that can increase your risk of disease, disability, and even death. According to Dr Frank Booth, professor at the University of Missouri, physical inactivity is a primary cause of most chronic diseases. It's important to work with a doctor to find the best types of physical activity to help you maintain your health and mobility.

There are four key physical components to ensuring overall good health, fitness, and mental well-being:

- Cardiovascular / Aerobic conditioning
- Strength training and muscular development
- Stretching – muscles, ligaments and tendons
- Mental rest and relaxation – balanced lifestyle

Finding ways to reduce stress is another strategy that can help you stay healthy. You may want to try meditation, mindfulness, yoga, relaxation music, and taking vacations (see Chapter 7 for more information about coping with stress and emotions). Based on studies conducted by Divya Krishnakumar, the author of the research 'Meditation and Yoga can Modulate Brain Mechanisms that affect Behavior and Anxiety – A Modern Scientific Perspective', the practice of meditation triggers neurotransmitters that modulate psychological disorders such as anxiety. When you mindfully exercise, you increase the availability of brain chemicals that promote new brain connections, reduce stress, and improve sleep. And when we sleep, we reduce stress hormones that can be harmful to the brain and clear out proteins that injure it.

A BALANCED DIET

Although you may have heard many contradictory claims about the best diets and ways to lose weight, most healthcare professionals advocate a simple, balanced diet rather than a strict diet plan that restricts certain foods. It's important to ensure that your body receives all the nutrients it needs and isn't being saturated with unhealthy, sugary, and salty foods. Eating balanced meals three times a day and keeping hydrated will ensure your body is healthy, and it will also improve other aspects such as your mental health, concentration, and productivity.

The Mediterranean diet meets many of the criteria for good health. This diet is rich in olive oil, fruits, vegetables, nuts and fish, low in red and processed meats, and includes a moderate amount of cheese and wine. There is convincing evidence that it's effective at warding off heart attacks, stroke, and premature death.

You may be inspired by the four 'Golden Rules' for a good diet put forward by Eric Edmeades, founder of the WildFit program:

1. Diets that work should be sustainable. This means that a diet should not be a short-term shift that makes you miserable (classic yo-yo diet) and involves insane willpower. Rather than fighting to cut out unhealthy food, it's better to enjoy healthy alternatives. This eliminates the need to use willpower and allows you to retain your ideal body forever. It's about changing mindset and your relationship with food.

2. Diets that work should be nutritious. We all need nutritional requirements such as proteins, fats, calcium, iron, vitamins, omega-3s, etc. According to Eric Edmeades, food companies stuff their products with unnecessary ingredients, and most of these additives are extremely bad for our health. When we eat foods with no nutritional value, our body struggles to even register this as food, because it's not receiving the nutrients needed to power itself properly. It signals to the brain that more food is needed. Sugar is the biggest culprit. Not only are sugars quickly converted into body fat, they also trigger our appetite, which is why most diets that work recommend eliminating as much sugar as possible.

3. Diets that work include fewer calories than you burn off to lose weight.

4. Diets that work take your lifestyle into account. Your genetics and daily lifestyle should play an important role in the weight loss program that works for you. For example, a professional athlete will need more calories than other people. A person with a food intolerance or some other form of health problem will need a diet to be adjusted accordingly. That's why it's worth speaking with a professional nutritionist about major changes to your diet.

MENTAL HEALTH

In their article 'Toward a new definition of mental health' (2015, World Psychiatry), Galderisi, Heinz, Kastrup, Beezhold, and Sartorius proposed the following definition of mental health:

Mental health is a dynamic state of internal equilibrium which enables individuals to use their abilities in harmony with universal values of society. Basic cognitive and social skills; ability to recognize, express and modulate one's own emotions, as well as empathize with others; flexibility and ability to cope with adverse life events and function in social roles; and harmonious relationship between body and mind represent important components of mental health which contribute, to varying degrees, to the state of internal equilibrium.

The concept of mental health is related to the social and emotional well-being of individuals and communities. Having good mental health, or being mentally healthy, goes beyond the realms of the absence of illness; rather, it's a state of overall well-being and relates to:

- Getting enjoyment from life.
- Coping and "bouncing back" from stress and sadness.
- Being able to set and fulfill goals.
- Having the capability to build and maintain relationships with others.

Mental health is influenced by several biological, psychological, social, and environmental factors which interact in complex ways. These include individual factors such as the ability to manage thoughts and cope with stressors, and having communication and social skills to support connection with others. It also includes structural factors such as safe living environments, employment, education, freedom from discrimination and violence, and access to economic resources. It's also related to community factors such as a positive sense of belonging, community connectedness, and participation in society.

Mental health has an impact on life expectancy. Living a healthy lifestyle is important for anyone who wants to feel their best and remain in good health as they grow older. Every person's body works differently, so there isn't necessarily an ideal lifestyle. However, adopting certain habits can contribute to longevity.

WHAT IS THE SECRET TO LONGEVITY?

Longevity refers to living for a long time in comparison to others of the same species. You may think that your genes determine your longevity, but the truth is genetics account for at most 30% of your life expectancy. The rest comes from your behaviors, attitudes, environment, and a little bit of luck. Dan Buettner advanced the concept of "Blue Zones": there are some parts of the world where people live measurably longer lives than others (e.g. the Greek island Icaria; the province of Ogliastra, Sardinia; Okinawa, Japan; and the Nicoya Peninsula, Costa Rica). According to research, cultural, environmental, dietary, and spiritual practices are contributing factors to extraordinary longevity.

No matter your age, following these strategies will improve your chances of living a longer, healthier life:

- Find purpose: Creating meaning in life brings happiness and greater health. University College London found that among more than 9,000 people over the age of 65, those who had the greatest sense of purpose in their life were 30% less likely to die during the next eight years than those with the lowest sense of purpose. When you wake up in the morning, create something meaningful to do or work towards. When you have something to live for, you just might end up sticking around a little longer.

- Have faith: Knowing that you have some divine help will get you through the toughest of times. Reach out for help when you need it.
- Stay social: Nurture your relationships and connect with others. A healthy social life will keep your mind and body active. Keep family and loved ones close by for support and guidance.
- Get involved and join in: Being part of a group with common interests provides a sense of belonging, so find out about local sporting, music, volunteer, or community groups.
- Relax: Don't underestimate the importance of downtime. Rest, meditate, and do things that don't create stress.
- Stretch: Take up dance or yoga, which can increase flexibility while at the same time providing a stress-reducing mind-body experience.
- Move: Avoid sitting all day. The lack of stimulus to the muscles can produce harmful effects such as an increased risk of heart disease, diabetes, and many forms of cancer like breast and colon. Sitting all day slows down the body's metabolism so fewer calories are burned, and levels of blood sugar and cholesterol can increase. Try taking a short walk every hour or two.
- Run: Running helps burn off calories and keep blood sugar levels normal, which is important because they keep your kidneys, eyes, nerves, and blood vessels healthy. Running also regulates blood pressure, increases lung capacity, reduces stress, and increases bone density.
- Manage stress: Taking deep breaths, taking care of your body, making time to unwind, and connecting with others can help to manage stress levels.
- Eat less: Follow the Japanese way of eating. In addition to eating lots of vegetables and fish, do not eat until the point you are completely full. Eat slowly and stop when you are about 80% full. According to Dr Edward Howell, author of Enzyme Nutrition,

we have a limited number of enzymes to break down the foods we eat. Eating smaller quantities helps to use fewer enzymes, thereby prolonging life.
- Eat more vegetables and fruit: High fiber diets have been found to promote lower cholesterol levels and reduce the risk of heart disease and certain cancers such as colon cancer. Ensure you include berries in your diet. Berry fruits have received considerable attention due to their high concentrations of antioxidant and anti-inflammatory phytochemicals. Dr Shukitt-Hale says, "These phytochemicals have the ability to alter cellular function by reducing oxidative and inflammatory stressors. Their bioactive properties have the potential to prevent or delay brain aging."
- Eat more plant protein: Plant proteins (e.g. tofu, lentils, chickpeas, peanuts, almonds, spirulina, quinoa, chia seeds, beans, potatoes, broccoli) supply all nine amino acids the body can't make on its own. Unlike animal proteins, plant-based proteins can help lower blood pressure, reduce the risk of heart disease, and decrease the risk of cancer.
- Drink wine: Red wine has antioxidants, polyphenols, and flavonoids that are very beneficial for the heart. It's good for overall health, protection from heart disease, and decreasing inflammation.
- Implement a diet rich in omega-3: Omega-3 rich foods such as fish (salmon, mackerel, sardines), flaxseeds, walnuts, tofu, and spinach may add years to your life.
- Avoid smoking: Smoking causes internal damage to your genetic code as well as blood vessels and multiple organ systems.
- Drink coffee: Some research indicates that moderate coffee intake may help fight Type 2 diabetes, and may even reduce the risk of dementia and heart disease.
- Get quality sleep: Sleep for at least seven to eight hours every night. Sleep affects our physical and mental health, but can be the

first thing we trade in when we get busy or stressed. Poor sleep can lead to all kinds of health problems, from obesity and heart disease to depression. Good sleep can help your energy levels, cognitive function, and personal relationships. So, you don't just live a longer life, you feel good and live a better-quality life.

- Get more of the "sunshine" vitamin D: Getting 15 to 30 minutes of sun exposure a day should be adequate for vitamin D production. It has been shown to fight disease, improve bone health, and ward off depression.
- Have sex: It releases oxytocin, the "feel-good hormone", reduces stress, and lowers blood pressure.
- Keep your brain active: Your brain also needs some exercise, so give it a mental workout to reduce the risk of dementia and Alzheimer's. Constantly learning new things or expanding our knowledge also helps tremendously. Problem-solving keeps the brain working.
- Think positively: Be optimistic, concentrate on the good rather than the bad things, avoid negative self-talk, and practice gratitude.
- Take time out for things you enjoy: Balance in life is important, so taking time out for things you enjoy can make a difference to how you think and feel.

How many practices on that list do you follow? Do you take care of your physical body and spirit or live a stressed existence without enough time in the day, surrounded by the wrong people, without enough emphasis on your own well-being? The more stressed and unfulfilled we feel, the more it shows in our appearance. Without slowing down, there isn't time to cook healthy meals, exercise, and practice prayer or meditation. You still have the rest of life's journey ahead of you. You're only as old as you feel. Wanting to feel young enough to create new and exciting experiences is a dynamic that can occur at any age…and does.

CHECK IN

The above suggestions for physical activity, a balanced diet, mental health, and longevity could represent a lot of lifestyle changes, even for the most dedicated of people. To make achieving change more accessible, check in with yourself by asking the following questions as a starting point:

1. Does your diet include fresh fruit and vegetables, and provide you with enough energy?
2. Do you avoid having too much alcohol?
3. Do you exercise for 30 minutes at least three times per week?
4. Do you get enough sleep?
5. Do you have a vacation or enjoy time off at least once a year?

FINDING INNER BALANCE

In order to create a healthy, balanced lifestyle, you need to make small adjustments to your daily routine. Recalibrate your mind and body to ensure well-being. Start each day with a habit of success. Get up and move your body more often for the physical and mental benefits. Meditate to center yourself every day. Living a healthy lifestyle doesn't need to be complicated. As Wilhelm von Humboldt once said, "True enjoyment comes from activity of the mind and exercise of the body; the two are ever united."

SUMMARY

This chapter was designed to give you some strategies which you can adapt and experiment with throughout your life to develop good habits and become capable of taking the required measures to lead a healthy and active lifestyle. In particular, you have discovered strategies towards encouraging longevity. No matter your age, you can take personal responsibility for your body and mind. You can always improve on your journey and select what works for you and what doesn't. Remember, you have one life; live it well.

REDO INNER BALANCE INVENTORY QUESTION

In three to six months, perhaps having applied some of the strategies learned in this chapter, go back and reassess the inner balance inventory question. How do you rate your health, mental condition, fitness, appearance, dietary habits, immune system, sleep quality, and concentration?

Write your rating and reflection here. Try not to make judgments, but an honest assessment of how you approach your health and well-being.

Rating on a scale of 1 to 10, with 1 being low and 10 being high:

1   2   3   4   5   6   7   8   9   10

Reflection:

CHAPTER

9

EMBRACING SPIRITUAL LIFE

Most humans are never fully present in the now, because unconsciously they believe that the next moment must be more important than this one. But then you miss your whole life, which is never not now.

Eckhart Tolle

INNER BALANCE INVENTORY QUESTION

Before we start exploring how to develop your spiritual life, take a moment to assess: do you regularly make time for any reflection, spiritual practice, meditation, or contemplation that helps you feel balanced and calm?

Write your rating and reflection here. Try not to make judgments, but an honest assessment of how much attention and care you put into your spiritual life?

Rating on a scale of 1 to 10, with 1 being low and 10 being high:

1   2   3   4   5   6   7   8   9   10

Reflection:

In the previous chapter, we reflected on how to take care of your health and well-being. You learned useful strategies that you can apply to leading a healthy and fit lifestyle. You also discovered habits that impact life expectancy, which you may want to adopt, and the extent to which cultural, environmental, dietary, and spiritual practices contribute to extraordinary longevity.

In this chapter, we move on to the ninth area of inner balance: spiritual life. The core of spirituality is finding alignment, and having a healthy body is part of enlarging our spiritual life. You will be guided through how to live in the present moment and practice self-reflection, and discover different tools for exploring spirituality to find more meaning and purpose in life.

We live in a very dynamic and high-pressure environment. More and more people are starting to realize how important spirituality is to maintaining a balanced life. To live a balanced life, we need to nurture our spirituality in whatever form it takes. Each of us has different needs and preferences, and you may find different ways to explore your spiritual life. However, there are many ways to enlarge our spiritual life and, at the same time, enhance our life more generally.

HOW IS SPIRITUALITY DEFINED?

Spirituality can be broadly defined as a sense of connection to something higher than ourselves. The sense of transcendence experienced in spirituality is a universal experience. Spirituality describes a much broader understanding of an individual's connection with the transcendent aspects of life. Some might find it in religion, while others may find it in meditation. Many people search for meaning in their lives. In spirituality, the key question is: where do I personally find meaning, connection, and value?

While the understanding of spirituality differs across religions and belief systems, it can be described as finding meaning and purpose in life. Spirituality is different for everyone, but the foundations required to achieve and maintain spiritual health and well-being are the same. Whether you attend regular religious services, study different religious texts, practice yoga or mindfulness, or look to a power within the universe higher than yourself, taking care of yourself spiritually is important. Seeking a meaningful connection with something bigger than yourself can result in increased positive emotions. The transcendent moments you experience can be filled with peace, wonder, gratitude, acceptance, and contentment. Let's look at some ways of exploring spirituality with intention.

REFLECTION

To reflect is to contemplate or ponder with serious thought and consideration. Reflection is the foundation of spirituality. When you spend time reflecting, you seek – and often find –answers. Through self-reflection, you pose the question: what is my purpose? By reflecting on your reason for existence or the meaning of life – specifically, your own personal journey on this Earth – you discover purpose. Life can be hard. No one denies that. A huge piece of spiritual wellness is how you deal with pain, anger, grief, suffering, and the things that happen to you and around you. Reflection allows us to find meaning in these events and to accept both the good and the bad, appreciating all life's experiences. Regularly reflecting on your personal values and beliefs is the foundation to a grounded spiritual practice.

MINDFULNESS: PRACTICE LIVING IN THE PRESENT MOMENT

Like other reflective practices, mindfulness can be a tool to discover how spirituality manifests in your life. Mindfulness teaches you to be aware of what is happening in your body and mind in the present moment and to be open to it with curiosity and kindness. This allows you to explore beliefs, perspectives, and experiences in a way that might lead to new insights around spiritual questions. Mindfulness helps you focus and ignore the distractions around you. It also helps to hone your ability to notice more in your environment. This gives you access to the present moment with a fuller perspective on your experience.

Anyone can start a mindful practice of meditation to find a new level of calm. It's all about the discipline of sitting down and going inward. Mindfulness allows you to be in the present moment, a timeframe associated with feelings of happiness. It can increase your attention span, and combat a wandering mind and excessive self-referential thoughts. With over-activity, these unhealthy states of mind can lead to unhappiness. Managing your "monkey mind" (a metaphor for a confused, unsettled, and distracted mind) through daily meditation is a simple and easy first line of defense against endless modern-day distractions.

Mindful meditation can create physical changes in the brain through neuroplasticity (see Richard Widdett's (Western Michigan University) article, 'Neuroplasticity and Mindfulness Meditation').

This increasingly popular concept refers to the brain's ability to reorganize and change continuously throughout your lifespan. Behavior and lifestyle are major influencers on the brain. So, life events make your brain constantly create new neural connections. That is because neurons (nerve cells) actively adjust to compensate to changes in your environment.

According to Eckhart Tolle, a world-renowned spiritual teacher and author of the books *The Power of Now: A Guide to Spiritual Enlightenment* and *A New Earth: Awakening to Your Life's Purpose*, you can learn to live in the present moment and observe your state of mind by practicing the following:

1. Bring presence to everyday activities

Happiness isn't in the future or the past but in mindful awareness of the present. You can bring a conscious presence to the everyday activities that you do unconsciously; for example, washing your dishes, preparing a hot drink, brushing your teeth, or lying down in bed. Instead of indulging in thinking, these are all opportunities for being there as a still, alert presence. Breathe; feel the energy inside your body. Even the busiest person has time for 60 seconds of space.

2. Bring presence to your relationships

Giving your full attention and being present is the greatest gift you can give someone. It's especially important for parents and children, but also in intimate relationships. Can you listen to the other person in that simple state of alertness in which you're not judging what you're listening to? If you do not impose mental labels, judgments, or definitions on the other person, you can achieve a deeper level of awareness.

3. Overcome worries

Worry is repetitive, negative thought patterns. There are three methods you can use to step out of the stream of negative thinking:

1. First, move into the present moment by taking a few deep breaths.
2. Second, place your attention on the feeling of aliveness in your body: in your hands, your arms, your legs, and so on.
3. Third, place all of your attention on an object in your environment.

Start by entering the present moment so you find that space in which problems cannot survive. In that moment, you contact a deeper intelligence than the conditioned thinking mind. That is the place where intuition, creative action, knowledge, and wisdom come from. Make sure you're not in a state of negativity with the present moment, because you can take action on the basis of negativity, which can bring weaker results.

4. Conquer negative self-talk

Most people are not aware that they have a voice in their heads that keeps talking and talking and with whom they completely identify. In many people's cases, the voice in their head is a predominantly unhappy one, so this unconscious internal dialogue continuously generates an enormous amount of negativity. We are not our thoughts. The very fact that we can objectively observe our thinking suggests that the constant, and often negative, dialogue in our heads is separate from who we really are. Realizing this can bring us closer to peace. Use these methods to overcome self-talk:

1. Take time out to reflect on your thoughts and inner voice.
2. Stop and say to yourself: "What's the thought? What is driving it? How am I feeling?"

3. Use concrete, positive affirmation. For instance, instead of saying, "I am never going to get this right," challenge the thought with, "I am doing my best, and my best is enough."
4. Shift perspectives. Try asking yourself, "How would my best friend respond to it?" or "Would I talk to my best friend the same way?"

5. Practice gratitude

Gratitude is an essential part of being present. When you go deeply into the present, gratitude arises spontaneously, even if it's just gratitude for breathing or the aliveness you feel in your body. Gratitude is there when you acknowledge the aliveness of the present moment; that's the foundation for successful living.

To enhance your spiritual life, it's important to find time for solitude, when you can quiet your mind and reconnect with yourself. Although you may not be able to stop difficult things happening in your life, you can control your reactions to them by reconnecting with your spirituality in a variety of ways and leading a more balanced, happier life.

REFLECTIVE TOOLS FOR EXPLORING SPIRITUALITY

MEDITATION

Meditation is a powerful way to incorporate spirituality in your life. Meditation can be done by yourself or with a group of people. It can help lower stress and create more balance in your life. Studies have even shown that people who meditate on a regular basis perform better at work and are more able to manage conflict in their lives. Meditation can induce feelings of calm and clear-headedness as well as improve concentration and attention. Brain researcher Richard Davidson has shown that meditation increases the brain's gray matter density, which can reduce sensitivity to pain, enhance your immune system, help you regulate difficult emotions, and relieve stress. Mindfulness meditation in particular has proven helpful for people with depression and anxiety, cancer, fibromyalgia, chronic pain, rheumatoid arthritis, Type 2 diabetes, chronic fatigue syndrome, and cardiovascular disease. You can learn more from Daniel Siegel, an internationally recognized expert on mindfulness and therapy, in his book *The Mindful Therapist: A Clinician's Guide to Mindsight and Neural Integration*.

Meditation helps us master our mind by working on our attention. By mastering our ability to intentionally direct our attention and keep it there, and removing our attention from anything that is negative or not serving us, we can begin to gain clarity about reality and our goals. In meditation, we don't typically use imagination or evoke emotions. Instead, we focus our attention either on a particular object or on observing the reality of the present moment, without any attempt to add to or alter it. The purpose is to quiet the mind and allow it to perceive reality for what it is. It brings us insight, enlightenment, and comfortable silence in the mind. With practice, mindfulness can leave us in a calmer, more stable, and enlightened state. You can start with as little as a minute a day and gradually increase the time you spend. Some people even notice that they have more time once they start meditating. Suddenly, they gain clarity about what is important in their day-to-day life and stop spending time on things that don't truly serve them.

Exercise: Eye of the hurricane meditation

I notice that many people struggle with the idea of "becoming aware of the present moment", which is at the heart of mindfulness practice. You might wish to try this mindfulness exercise created by psychologists Dr Hugo Alberts and Dr Lucinda Poole. This tool is designed to help you disengage from the hectic world around you by focusing your attention inward. It uses the metaphor of a hurricane to guide you to a state in which you become an observer who is able to notice what is happening from moment to moment with a sense of calm and clarity.

In this meditation, the concept of inner peace is presented using a hurricane metaphor. Within the strong, turbulent winds of a hurricane is the eye: a calm, quiet, centered space. The goal of this exercise is help you to explore inner peace by using your breath to become like the eye of the hurricane. By connecting to your breath, you can disconnect from upsetting thoughts, emotions, and other stressors that disrupt inner peace.

Find a comfortable meditation position and follow the instruction created by Dr Hugo Alberts and Dr Lucinda Poole: https://www.youtube.com/watch?v=HPFayxlm_ms

When you feel ready, slowly open your eyes and reflect for a moment:

- How do you feel after practicing this exercise?
- What kind of experiences did you notice?
- Did the eye of the hurricane metaphor resonate with you? If not, can you think of another metaphor that would resonate with you more?

YOGA

Yoga is a centuries-old spiritual practice that aims to create a sense of union within the practitioner through physical postures, ethical behaviors, and breath expansion. Yoga is a physical technique that can help improve your spiritual wellness by reducing emotional and physical strains on your mind and body. Yoga is taught at various different levels and can help lower stress, boost the immune system, and lower blood pressure as well as reduce anxiety, depression, fatigue, and insomnia.

Instead of simply being, often we are busy analyzing our actions and focusing on our physical performance. Is it possible to develop awareness without taking the time and space to connect deeper within yourself? Yoga gives the space to do just that. Many teachers will speak of the importance of the quiet mind. Push yourself through the highly physical postures in order to be exhausted enough to go into your quiet mind or sacred inner space. Experience being. Don't expect positivity, peacefulness or happiness but, if they happen, be aware of what you experience, and be grateful. Being able to take this feeling of gratitude and surrender into your everyday life away from the mat makes yoga a spiritual practice.

Most of us are busy with job commitments, clients, children; we can spend a lot of time in our heads. Our minds are often processing hundreds of tasks and thoughts: our endless to-do list. This can cause a lot of stress and fatigue to our adrenal glands, according to Jeffery Dusek, PhD, chief research officer at Kripalu Center for Yoga & Health in Stockbridge, Massachusetts. Yoga quiets the mind by offering time and space to connect deeper within yourself and your body. Why not try out some slow rhythmic breathing practices and meditative/relaxation practices in a yoga class to help ground yourself and find presence, inducing an overall sense of calm, well-being, stress tolerance, and mental focus.

JOURNALING

Journaling is another contemplative practice that can help you become more aware of your inner life and feel more connected to your experience and the world around you. Studies show that writing during difficult times may help you find meaning in life's challenges and become more resilient in the face of obstacles. Journaling is a powerful tool for self-development and spiritual growth. It's a way to learn about yourself and develop a relationship with your inner world, by applying an analytical mind.

When is the best time to practice journaling?

- When you feel disconnected.
- When you are lost.
- When you feel overwhelmed.
- When you are searching for the solution to a problem.
- When you want to find clarity.
- When you are caught up in difficult emotions.
- When you want to find calm.

Journaling is an inner process of self-discovery. It's contemplative, focusing on the emotional or spiritual landscape. It's worth exploring more about the journaling process and the idea behind starting your day with the "morning pages" from *The Artist's Way* by Julia Cameron. The technique is to write freely, without judgment, about absolutely anything that comes to mind in the morning. It helps you get clarity, prioritize things, and synchronize your day. Journaling usually develops your analytical and intuitive side. You can investigate causes of stress, and break down the issue into actionable steps. You can reflect on decision-making, behaviors, mindset, obligations, experienced events, including an overview of your emotions, thoughts, insights, or anything else that stands out. Transferring thoughts, fantasies, worries or dreams to the page is an act of alchemy. You can also ask yourself a lot of questions on the page, and respond intuitively. Asking the right questions is an art, and much is revealed by asking the tough questions, the ones you may feel reluctant to answer.

FINDING INNER BALANCE

Everyone needs to set aside time for themselves when they can be completely alone. This preferably means finding an area where you can be alone with yourself in silence without distractions and disconnect from the world. It has been noted that today people have shorter attention spans than ever before. To enlarge your spiritual life, it's important to find time for solitude: a time to let go of stress and regrets, and reconnect with yourself. Although you may not be able to stop bad things happening in your life, you can work on controlling your reactions to them. By reconnecting with your spirituality in a variety of ways (practicing meditation, yoga, journaling, reflection, or being present), you can lead a more balanced, happier life.

SUMMARY

In this chapter, you have learned about other important skills on your journey. You have discovered how to live in the present moment, practice and observe your state of mind, and bring a conscious presence to everyday activities. Bring presence to your relationships by listening more consciously and with full awareness. Overcome worries and negative thinking by practicing breathing, gratitude, and finding solitary time for yourself. You were also reminded about the benefits of practicing meditation, yoga, journaling or any other form of activity to help you ignore unwanted distractions in your life, be more present and improve concentration. By reflecting and finding more meaning, balance and calm in your life, you can improve your mental health and decrease pain, worries, and also depression.

REDO INNER BALANCE INVENTORY QUESTION

In three to six months, perhaps having applied some of the strategies learned in this chapter, go back and reassess the inner balance inventory question. Ask yourself: do you regularly make time for reflection, spiritual practice, meditation or contemplation that helps you feel balanced and calm?

Write your rating and reflection here. Try not to make judgments, but an honest assessment of how much attention and care you put into your spiritual life.

Rating on a scale of 1 to 10, with 1 being low and 10 being high:

1   2   3   4   5   6   7   8   9   10

Reflection:

CHAPTER 10

EXPANDING YOUR INTELLECTUAL CAPACITY

I'm passionately involved in life: I love its change, its colour, its movement. To be alive, to be able to see, to walk, to have houses, music, paintings – it's all a miracle.

Arthur Rubinstein

INNER BALANCE INVENTORY QUESTION

Before we start exploring how to expand your intellectual life, take a moment and think: to what extent do you feel you are constantly developing, broadening your horizons, and gaining new skills? Do you find time for reading, listening to music, or learning something new?

Write your rating and reflection here. Try not to make judgments, but an honest assessment of what you currently do to expand your intellectual capacity.

Rating on a scale of 1 to 10, with 1 being low and 10 being high:

1   2   3   4   5   6   7   8   9   10

Reflection:

In the previous chapter, we explored methods to encourage living in the present moment, practicing and observing our state of mind, and bringing a conscious presence to our everyday activities. We discovered different tools for exploring spirituality to find more meaning and purpose in life. In this chapter, we will focus on the tenth area of inner balance: expanding your intellectual capabilities. We will investigate how to enhance our personal growth, including developing curiosity, learning new skills, and broadening our horizons.

INVEST IN YOURSELF

Intellectual life is about thoughts, knowledge, and ideas. To expand your intellectual life, you have to invest in yourself. The greater your time investment in reading, learning new things, and meeting and talking to interesting people, the more you will expand your intellectual journey. Improving yourself is the best way to grow your professional career and your personal life. You can either embrace different ways to broaden your intellectual life and stand out, or end up feeling frustrated that you did not try. The good news is that time invested in your own personal growth is completely under your own control.

Our brain is a thinking and learning superpower. And we can use it for free and with great benefit if we know how to acquire and apply knowledge and skills. We live at a time of unlimited access to knowledge, including well-designed courses (many of them for free), and we are surrounded by people who are willing to share their experiences and ideas for the benefit of others. We can learn how to improve our brainpower to become more successful, communicate better, make smarter decisions, make more money, and expand our intellect too.

Expanding your horizons opens the world to you by introducing you to new possibilities. Novel experiences may invite the unfamiliar into your life, bringing you diverse experiences, which broadly increase your knowledge. The brain responds to new things by creating new neural pathways and, with repetition, each new pathway becomes stronger, giving us new skills and strengths. For this purpose, you should always try to stay slightly outside your comfort zone (see Chapter 2). This can be accomplished in many different ways, such as taking a different route home, trying new food, visiting an art gallery or a botanical garden instead of watching TV, or listening to an audiobook in the car. The brain is formed around habits. The more rigid and habituated you are, the harder it is to cope with change. Whatever is routine in your life actually keeps you from growing in the ways you could if you did just a few things differently on a daily basis. Try to experiment more and train yourself to thrive in new ways, with new people, and in new environments.

FIVE SIMPLE WAYS TO EXPAND YOUR INTELLECTUAL CAPABILITIES

1. IMPROVE CONCENTRATION

A recent study by Microsoft concluded that the average human attention span has dropped to just eight seconds, shrinking nearly 25% in just a few years. With that kind of attention span, you can't achieve anything spectacular or worthwhile in life. Learning how to build a longer attention span is one of the key priorities to begin with. There are various learning techniques you can apply to improve your working memory. If you optimize your working memory wisely, you may have fewer problems learning, focusing, understanding, reading, memorizing, organizing yourself, meeting deadlines, and remembering or keeping track of things. In order to optimize your working memory, try challenging yourself to work in a flow without distractions for a specific time slot (90 minutes preferably) and take regular breaks (for more inspiration go back to Chapter 4). It's better to start with your most difficult tasks. Avoid multitasking; concentrate on one thing at a time, starting with the most important. Moreover, it's also very important to create a positive mindset and, as far as possible, eliminate the negative thoughts and emotions that might distract you.

2. DEVELOP CURIOSITY

Curiosity is one of the most important values to develop and nurture if you want to expand your intellectual life. With curiosity, you can easily engage your mind in things, commit to understanding, acquire new knowledge, and deliver better outcomes. Curiosity helps you think outside the box and develop a habit of using what you know in a new, more productive way. In the next section you will learn more about how to develop curiosity.

3. TRAIN YOUR LEFT AND RIGHT BRAIN

Whether you're a more creative or a more analytical person, you have to train both types of thinking. When both hemispheres of the brain work at their full potential and in harmony, you will get the most out of your intellect. There are a number of useful exercises that can help you train your left and right brain hemispheres:

- There are many applications that provide games and problem-solving techniques designed to increase the neuroplasticity of our brain. Neuroplasticity is the brain's ability to form new neural connections, enabling us to function at a higher level. The more neuroplasticity your brain has the faster it makes new connections and the quicker and more effectively you process information.
- Draw ideas and things and discover new connections and new connotations. You might even start by asking yourself and others thousands of questions like a curious child.
- Write down hundreds of ideas and do not assess them negatively.
- Play with ideas and concepts in a ridiculous way, experiment, test things immediately, do the usual things differently, or try new things.

4. BE IMAGINATIVE

Most successes begin as imagined outcomes, opportunities, and possibilities. As long as you allow yourself to be imaginative, you will be able to create innovative and effective problem-solving strategies. The more visionary you become, the more familiar you will be with drawing inspiration from all areas of life when the opportunity arises. Try starting with reading, as it gives us a break, puts us into another world, and creates an emotional connection between us and the words on the page. It can provide a good way to escape from daily life: if we are not able to take a vacation, reading a book can be a great substitute and provide training for building imagination skills.

5. NEVER STOP LEARNING NEW SKILLS

Active learning is significantly more efficient than passive learning (see 'A Controlled Trial of Active Versus Passive Learning' by Paul Haidet, et al). On average, you only get a 5% benefit from listening to lectures, and only 10% while reading. This is why the world's best universities place a lot more emphasis on intellectual discussions and other forms of learning. Discussions are an incredibly effective way of learning, especially if the group members have completely diverse experiences and hold different beliefs that challenge our point of view. Spend time with smart, interesting people and interact with them. Exchange your thoughts and ideas. Find focus groups on a subject you are interested in, or something completely new, and try to interact with them even if you are not an expert. It takes time to learn new things, but you can do it if you have a little bit of courage and faith in yourself. Remember, progress makes us happy. According to Jim Kwik, brain coach and author of *Limitless*, even the smallest step in the right direction can lead to the biggest leap of your life. Activity can increase the learning process: for example, by connecting what you are reading with other content you have read and your own life experience. Or if you apply information you have read, or if somebody physically demonstrates how to do something, you will remember significantly more than if you just read about it or saw it on a video. This is why mentoring programs are so successful and beneficial towards increasing our competencies.

Examples:

- Learning a foreign language gives your brain a good workout. It's one of the most effective and practical ways to increase intelligence, keep your mind sharp, and has the added benefit of increased tolerance, because in learning a new language you also learn about the culture in which the language operates.
- Learning how to play a musical instrument can enhance verbal memory, spatial reasoning, and literacy skills. Playing an instrument makes you use both sides of your brain, which strengthens memory power.
- Learning from others' experiences by reading autobiographies and biographies gives you a different perspective and can be an inspiration for your own life. It can lead you to a greater understanding of the world as well as better decision-making by incorporating some of the solutions and lessons you learn.

DEVELOP CURIOSITY

You can develop your intellectual curiosity using the following steps:

Step 1: Start exploring a new subject

Recognizing gaps in your knowledge can give you some direction as to what you should learn about going forwards. Research has shown that the brain responds to new things by creating new neural pathways. Each new pathway becomes stronger with repetition, extending our new skills and strengths.

Step 2: Ask questions

Getting answers to questions is a stepping stone in developing intellectual curiosity. Use the "Five Whys" technique and ask "why?" five times consecutively to identify the root of a problem.

Step 3: Do what interests you

Following your interests and passions keeps you invested in the continuous learning process more naturally.

Step 4: Familiarize yourself with diverse topics

Having a diverse knowledge base helps you think about a subject from multiple angles. Exposing the mind to opposing ideas expands its horizons and your ability to grasp different points of view, contributing to a more tolerant and open-minded attitude useful in negotiations in all walks of life.

Step 5: Learn from past experiences

Without training ourselves to learn from our past experiences, we tend to fall into old habits and repeat the same mistakes. Ask yourself what you learned from a particular experience. What would you do differently next time?

Step 6: Learn from others

Besides learning from other people, it also gives you an opportunity to be inspired and work on developing your skills.

In order to expand your intellectual life, you need to find pleasure in your pursuits and time for personal growth. Think for a moment about what you like to do to expand your horizons. Ask yourself which new thing you would like to try out to make your life richer. It might also help to remind yourself:

- When did you last go to a concert, the opera, the theater, or a musical?
- When did you last read for fun?
- When did you last connect with somebody on an intellectual level?
- Have you visited a museum recently?
- Which club or society do you interact with currently?
- What skills did you master this year (e.g. learning a new language, learning how to play an instrument, dancing, singing, a new sporting activity)?
- What course or program did you take in a new discipline (e.g. technology, science, politics, art)?

- Which research program have you explored recently?
- When did you last have the chance to explore a new culture?
- When was the last time you discovered something fascinating, different, or delightful?

You'll never overcome your personal intellectual growth challenges purely by thinking about them. You need to take action and apply what you have learned. So today think about how much you want to explore new things in life and what specifically those will be.

FINDING INNER BALANCE

Intellectual growth means feeding your mind, gaining new skills, and being inspired to always keep learning. Be passionate about acquiring and developing new skills. To be a successful person, you must always search for what is new and not yet fully understood, staying on the cutting edge of your industry. As you may remember from Chapter 1, it all starts with your vision of life: how do you want to live your life? What will bring you the most happiness? From there you can determine the habits you need to develop, the skills and knowledge you want to master, and the step-by-step goals you need to achieve to get there.

It's humbling to grasp how much there still is to know. Learning how to continue your personal growth is essential to expanding your intellectual capacity, building your confidence, reaching your goals, and finding fulfillment. The more knowledge you acquire, the more information you have available to you when making critical decisions. For every hour you spend learning something, spend another hour applying what you have just learned to make best use of it.

SUMMARY

In this chapter, you have learned about expanding your intellectual capacity as another major skill on your journey. It's important to develop intellectual curiosity and plant the seeds for your own intellectual growth. The key lesson learned from this chapter is that if you want to expand your horizons and try something intellectually new, it's not enough to just think and read about it. You have to take action, apply what you have learned, and test out whether you like it. By expanding your horizons, you will unlock new possibilities.

REDO INNER BALANCE INVENTORY QUESTION

In three to six months, perhaps having applied some of the strategies in this chapter, go back and reassess the inner balance inventory question. Ask yourself: to what extent do you feel you are constantly developing, broadening your horizons, and gaining new skills? Do you find time for reading, listening to music, or learning something new?

Write your rating and reflection here. Try not to make judgments, but an honest assessment of what you currently do to expand your intellectual capacity.

Rating on a scale of 1 to 10, with 1 being low and 10 being high:

1   2   3   4   5   6   7   8   9   10

Reflection:

CHAPTER 11

PLANNING FINANCIAL FREEDOM

Financial freedom is available to those who learn about it and work for it.

Robert Kiyosaki

INNER BALANCE INVENTORY QUESTION

Before we explore the different ways to achieve financial freedom, take a moment to reflect: how financially secure are you? Do you have a consistent income, savings, good investments, loans to be paid?

Write your rating and reflection here. Try not to make judgments, but an honest assessment of your current level of financial security.

Rating on a scale of 1 to 10, with 1 being low and 10 being high:

1   2   3   4   5   6   7   8   9   10

Reflection:

In the previous chapter, we worked on developing intellectual curiosity and learning how to train our brain, in order to encourage personal growth, expand our horizons, and be ready for new possibilities. In this chapter, we will focus on the eleventh area of inner balance: planning financial freedom by gaining a better financial understanding and building healthy financial habits. It's about developing an "abundance mindset" and finding the right balance between working, saving, and enjoying your life.

If you're not sure how you think or feel about money, look around you. What do you see? How does it make you feel? What is your sense of financial security: do you have a consistent income, savings, good investments, or loans to be paid? What you have or don't have right now is a reflection of your thoughts, feelings, and beliefs about money. As T. Harv Eker, author of *Secrets of the Millionaire Mind*, said: "Money doesn't buy happiness, but it can buy freedom: freedom of choice, to be able to do what you enjoy doing and not be forced to do things just because you 'need the money.'"

The social isolation we've been experiencing during the pandemic has been a great teacher of the value of all relationships, whether that be our relationships with people, money, or both. At a time when we face many unknowns about what the future will bring, there's a great opportunity to think about life with gratitude. What matters is how grateful we are for what we have and how willing we are to share with others.

You might apply this to your finances and reflect on these questions:

- How do I feel about money?
- Do I have everything I want right now?
- Do I have everything I need to be happy?
- Am I worthy and deserving of having what I want?
- How do I feel about people who have a lot of money?
- Do I complain about money or do I accept responsibility for how much or how little I have?
- Do I spend every cent I make or do I use money to make more?
- Do I use money to support others?

BUILD HEALTHY FINANCIAL HABITS

The money decisions you make now can affect your finances for years to come. So, it's important to work on building healthy financial habits that will benefit you later. Developing good spending and saving habits, learning to budget, and investing wisely can help you avoid needless debt, put away money for the things that are important to you, and build wealth in the future. Here are eleven ideas to get you started:

1. Have a budget

Start by creating and following a budget to help you manage your money without stress. With a budget, you have permission to relax, since you know your priorities are accounted for. Your first step is to take a look at your income, and then decide when and how to spend your money. Once a week take five minutes to go over your budget and see whether your spending has stayed in line. Doing this regularly will give you a clear picture of whether or not you're meeting your spending goals for the month.

2. Balance your accounts

Regularly keeping track of the balance in your everyday account is so important. It can keep you from overdrawing your account and paying unnecessary late or overdraft fees, and even help you catch identity theft or see if someone has stolen your account information quickly.

3. Set financial goals

Having financial milestones in mind will help you keep your spending under control and reach your lifelong dreams. By setting long-term, mid-term, and short-term financial goals, you'll be one step closer to being financially secure. A long-term goal, for example, might be saving for retirement, while a short-term goal could be building up your emergency fund. Estimate how much money you'll need to meet each of your goals and be specific: actionable goals are much more likely to net results. Use an online savings calculator to work out how much you need to save each month to reach that goal within your set time frame. Keep track of how much you've saved towards each of your goals to remind yourself of your saving ability and dedication. Even if those amounts are small, they'll start adding up.

4. Pay yourself first

When you have money coming in, don't forget to pay yourself first. That means making savings a priority, not something you neglect until everything else is taken care of. Arrange for the money you're setting aside to be automatically transferred to your savings account. This makes saving easy and automatic. Just make sure to keep enough in your everyday account to pay your bills.

5. Plan your future

Take a moment to visualize and plan for your financial future. Create a plan that takes you through all of your major financial milestones, such as buying a home, paying for your children's education or even contributing to your retirement account. This will help you prioritize your goals and be more focused.

6. Research the market

Don't blindly follow the advice of friends, neighbors, or strangers. If someone suggests a good investment opportunity, don't blindly jump in. Research the facts for yourself and make sure you understand all aspects before investing. The more you know about an investment, market, or the people you are going into business with, the better the decisions you will make.

7. Shop smart

Know the difference between a want and a need to build a foundation for your wealth. If you can't manage your impulse control and distinguish between a want and a need now, you'll run into the problem of wasting your money on unnecessary purchases. First, become a smart shopper and think about whether you need the item at all before you buy it. That doesn't mean not buying things you want, but rather classifying wants and needs and ensuring that you have the money available to cover a purchase without dipping into savings. A good idea is to wait at least 24 hours before buying something big. You might find the urge passes. Another way of short-circuiting your impulse to buy is to work out how many hours of work the purchase price represents; chances are you'll think the item's not worth it.

8. Be ready for extra expenses

Irregular expenses may be things such as vacation spending, taxes or the illness of a family member. Take the time to identify these costs and plan for them. If you know that certain major expenses come once a year, set aside some money each month to cover them. By the time they come around again, you'll have saved enough in advance to pay for them without having to take from your savings or use a credit card. Aim to save the equivalent of three to six months' worth of expenses. That will cover you in the event of an emergency, such as sudden home repairs, losing your job, or dealing with an unexpected loss in the family.

9. Focus on career growth

Planning your career growth should include thinking about an adequate income. Keep your résumé updated so that when you hear of a good job opportunity, you can consider taking it. Continue to build your professional network, even if you stay in your current job. Well-built professional networks will create more opportunities to find an interesting job when you're ready for it as well as enhancing your current salary.

10. Use your benefits

For those who are employed, you may take advantage of your employee benefits as they are part of your compensation package and can bring tax benefits too. Health insurance may be paid with pre-tax earnings, so when it comes to retirement savings, be sure to take the employer matching contribution, if one is offered. It's basically free money for your retirement. Other employee benefits such as stock options or different insurance plans can also help you financially, depending on your situation.

11. Give back

Give back to your community in some way by making donations or contributions to the causes and charities you support, or by offering your time and talents instead. Regularly giving back will remind you to have gratitude for all that you have.

TRY THE SIX 'JARS' SYSTEM TO MANAGE MONEY

With a good, measurable, and balanced financial plan you can determine and meet your short- and long-term financial goals. Better financial understanding can give you a whole new approach to your budget and improve control over your financial freedom. To become a successful money manager, try T. Harv Eker's "Money Jars System". This technique uses six "jars" to manage your money:

- Necessities jar (55%) – rent, food, electricity, bills
- Financial freedom jar (10%) – stocks, mutual funds, real estate
- Long-term savings for spending jar (10%) – big purchases, vacations, rainy day fund
- Education jar (10%) – coaching, mentoring, books, courses
- Play jar (10%) – spoiling yourself and family, leisure expenses
- Give jar (5%) – charitable donations

1. Necessities

The necessities jar is your living jar, which you should put 55% of your money into. This money is for everyday living: food, housing, bills, gas, insurance, etc. If you need more than 55% of your money to live on, it's time to cut down on your spending or find ways to earn more.

2. Financial freedom account

The second jar is your freedom jar. Every time you receive money, you should put 10% of it into this jar. This should be your favorite jar, as it will only grow bigger and is not for everyday spending. You can use this money for investment in areas known as the "three pillars of wealth" (or assets): real estate, businesses, and the stock market. The goal of investing in assets is that eventually they'll create enough passive income for you when you're not working. The more you put in this jar, the more you'll have for the future.

3. Long-term savings for spending

The 10% in this jar is for future expenses (big purchases, vacations, rainy day fund, children's education). Monthly saving can add up to a large amount later and is especially important when retirement time comes, so better to start saving from today and spend later.

4. Education

Remember that education is always worth it, so invest 10% of your money in this jar. This money is for your personal growth: take any course or workshop that you're interested in. You never lose when you invest in growing your knowledge and improving your skills. Keep moving forwards!

5. Play

Use up money in this jar every month to prevent you playing too much or not playing at all. As you've been working hard all month, give yourself a little reward equivalent to 10% of your monthly income. This jar might help you improve your quality of life as your income increases.

6. Give

Too many of us forget this jar. As you're much better now at managing your finances, spend time and money helping others. Donate 5% of your monthly income to help people in need or simply buy your friends or family a gift on a special occasion. Giving inspires giving and you may make the world a better place.

SHAPE A POSITIVE MONEY MINDSET

Your money mindset is your personal beliefs about and attitude towards money. It can affect how you save, spend, and manage your money. If you have a positive money mindset, you don't feel the need to compare yourself to others; you enjoy helping others; you have the freedom to spend, but you don't have to; and you are able to achieve your financial goals. Your money mindset doesn't just focus on your wallet; it can touch all parts of your life, including your mental health, family, job, friendships, and relationships.

When you have a positive money mindset, you:

- Look for opportunities instead of seeing roadblocks.
- Recognize that every financial situation is fixable.
- See the value in asking for help.
- Accept that small steps add up to progress.
- Turn your attention away from what's wrong and focus on opportunities for success.
- Determine your actions and results when managing money.

In order to change your money mindset, you need to be willing to admit fault and replace any wrong ideas and values you associate with money. If you're not willing to give up limiting assumptions, you'll never be able to grow beyond them. It's also critical not to get into the habit of letting old mistakes hold you back. Even if you made a financial mistake some time ago, the best thing you can do is use what you have learned from that experience to help you make better decisions now and in the future. Learn to adopt the abundance mindset: believe that you have enough and there is enough to go around. Do not let a scarcity mindset enter your world, as this will perpetuate the idea that there is never enough, no matter how hard you try. This can make you jealous of others, cause anxiety, increase stress, and make your life miserable. Don't waste your time comparing yourself to others. Better to compare yourself to where you were a year ago to see your actual growth. Your money mindset can change how you think about yourself. It's very important to believe in yourself and appreciate how much you are worth and deserve. With a bit of confidence, you have the power to make your own success.

Change takes time. Changing your mindset about money may feel unnatural at first. It will feel like you are going against years of habit and tradition. When you're having a hard time living your new money mindset, make sure you don't go back to old bad habits. Be fully committed to your goals and dreams. Your goals should be a reflection of who you want to become, not who you are now. By stretching yourself and aiming to achieve the biggest dreams you have, you give yourself room to grow and improve. When you limit yourself with small, short-sighted goals, you limit your potential and growth.

FINDING INNER BALANCE

By building healthy financial habits, you can find the right balance between working, saving, and enjoying your life. It's OK to treat yourself – just make sure that you properly plan ahead and you're saving enough of your income to be comfortable. Financial stress is a result of not knowing how to manage money well. One thing all wealthy people have in common is good money management. Keeping track of where money goes is a key to financial success. And of course, remember: money won't buy happiness, but it does buy freedom and it can make life a little (or a lot) easier. Rather than thinking about what you can buy or get with your money, focus instead on what you can do with it. Money is there to help you live the life you want.

SUMMARY

In this chapter, you learned how to alter your relationship with money to empower you to reach your goals, build healthy financial habits, manage finances better, and reduce financial stress. When your relationship with money changes, your life will transform as well. So, what is stopping you from achieving everything you want in life?

REDO INNER BALANCE INVENTORY QUESTION

In three to six months, perhaps having applied some of the strategies learned in this chapter, go back and reassess the inner balance inventory question. Ask yourself: how financially secure are you? Do you have a consistent income, savings, good investments, loans to be paid?

Write your rating and reflection here. Try not to make judgments, but an honest assessment of your current financial security.

Rating on a scale of 1 to 10, with 1 being low and 10 being high:

1   2   3   4   5   6   7   8   9   10

Reflection:

CHAPTER 12

IMPROVING YOUR QUALITY OF LIFE

There is a way of living that has a certain grace and beauty. It is not a constant race for what is next, rather, an appreciation of that which has come before. There is a depth and quality of experience that is lived and felt, a recognition of what is truly meaningful. These are the feelings I would like my work to inspire. This is the quality of life that I believe in.

Ralph Lauren

INNER BALANCE INVENTORY QUESTION

Before we move on to the last area of inner balance, take a few minutes and think: how satisfied are you with the quality of your lifestyle and your living space? Who and what do you surround yourself with? Do you celebrate the important moments in your life?

Write your rating and reflection here. Try not to make judgments, but an honest assessment of your quality of life.

Rating on a scale of 1 to 10, with 1 being low and 10 being high:

1   2   3   4   5   6   7   8   9   10

Reflection:

In the previous chapter, we explored how to gain financial freedom by building healthy financial habits and finding the right balance between working, saving, and enjoying life. In this chapter we will focus on the twelfth area of inner balance: quality of life. In Chapter 1, you created your life vision, you sorted out your values, you selected your goals. Moving from each chapter to the next in this book, you have evaluated and acknowledged each step of your journey. You have followed a structured process towards building a better, more balanced and successful life. Now you have the chance to contemplate your overall quality of life. You may want to take another look at all the other areas of inner balance and see what quality you can add to each category.

YOU ARE THE ARCHITECT OF YOUR LIFE

With confidence, you can increase your chances of creating the life you want to live. Your mindset has everything to do with success. Even if we feel fear and have the tendency to self-sabotage, having the right mindset can enable us to overcome anything and achieve what we want. Your everyday beliefs determine the way you feel and act, and shape your quality of life. You are the architect of your life. You build the foundation and you choose the steps on your journey. You create the structure within which to manage your time, energy, and healthy habits. You shape your career and the relationships you trust. You choose abundance. Though you might encounter obstacles on your way, you can ensure that they do not hold you back. Challenge yourself and move outside your comfort zone to make the outcomes you want possible. Once you are committed to your goals, you will find the best way to achieve them and, at the same time, create optimal balance and harmony in your life. As Margaret Young, a famous 1920s American singer and comedian, said: "Often people attempt to live their lives backwards. They try to have more things, or more money, in order to do more of what they want so that they will be happier. The way it actually works is the reverse. You must first be who you really are, then do what you need to do in order to have what you want".

WHAT IS 'QUALITY OF LIFE'?

An overall assessment of life is measured using the following dimensions: life satisfaction, feelings or emotional states, both positive and negative, with reference to a particular point in time and a sense of having meaning and purpose in life. Quality of life was defined in the World Health Organization's cross-cultural project as: "An individual's perception of their position in life, in the context of the culture and value systems in which they live, and in relation to their goals, expectations, standards, and concerns. It is a broad ranging concept, affected in a complex way by the person's physical health, psychological state, level of independence, social relationships and their relationships to salient features of their environment."

The quality-of-life concept covers all aspects of life: emotional, psychological, and social. Although the term encompasses primarily psychological components, it remains a multi-dimensional concept that has been taken from several fields, the most important of which are biology, medicine, psychology, and sociology, but also the social sciences, politics, economics, and the environment. We should also bear in mind that quality of life has an objective and a subjective connotation. The objective indicator includes personal wealth and possessions, level of safety, and health facilities, among others. Subjective indicators are manifested in happiness, satisfaction with life, positive social relations, awareness of other people's feelings, emotional control, internal behavioural control, and personal and social responsibility.

WHAT IS THE RELATIONSHIP BETWEEN LIFESTYLE AND QUALITY OF LIFE?

Lifestyle refers to large parts of our life, for instance, the way we think about and perceive life (our life attitudes, our perception of reality, and our quality of life) and the degree of happiness we experience through the different dimensions of our existence. Whereas quality of life is the degree to which an individual is healthy, comfortable, and able to participate in or enjoy life events. People's evaluations of their quality of life are made within the parameters of the possibilities they see for themselves and are therefore a fundamental component of their identity.

Very often lifestyle represents the material objects that exist in our life: cars, houses, brand-name clothes, exotic vacations. It's defined by the "buy" and "spend" decisions we make when we have the chance to make a choice about how to use our money. It relates to values, the people who surround us, our upbringing, fashion, or social media. I personally think that it's never too late to modify your lifestyle, and a healthy lifestyle plays a crucial role in promoting quality of life, enhancing physical and mental health, and also having a higher level of life satisfaction. The important question is:

- What is the underlying factor responsible for determining quality of life?
- Is quality of life determined by numerous factors which people can influence?

Think for a moment about your answers to these questions.

IMPROVE YOUR QUALITY OF LIFE

Reflect on the strategies below and apply as many as you can to your everyday life:

Find meaning and purpose in everything you do

Our lives become richer when we ask ourselves this question: how can we find meaning and purpose in everything we do? If we do this often enough, we challenge ourselves to reflect on those values daily in the choices we make, the thoughts we think, and the words we say. We might get distracted or go off track, but the more we connect with what matters most to us personally, the better our lives become. Having a sense of purpose makes life better. Research has shown that even towards the end of life, having a project that gives us a sense of purpose improves quality of life. As Oscar Wilde said: "To live is the rarest thing in the world. Most people exist, that is all."

Celebrate events in life

Every moment in life is worth celebrating. It's vital that we remind ourselves of the value of life and why it's worth celebrating, especially when we're feeling down. Stress, pressure, and busy schedules can get the best of us and make us forget to treasure life. It's the last stop on our journey, so let's learn how to appreciate life and treasure the little moments as well as the big ones. Remind yourself to be grateful for the little things and choose to have fun.

Cherish leisure time

Life is precious. How we choose to spend our leisure time is a very important decision. A vacation provides the opportunity to explore the world with family and friends and create amazing experiences to remember for a lifetime. There are many things to consider when choosing your destination and it takes meticulous planning to ensure you are going to the right place. Time away from our everyday life can be the key to longevity, happiness, and success.

Maintain healthy relationships

Life today is hectic. With many competing demands, there is so little quality time to share with those who matter most. Live by your values and consider carefully who you let into your inner circle. It should only be people who support and lift you up. Happiness is found in the quality of our relationships. Cultivating depth in those relationships comes from being willing to learn from others, appreciating the unique value they offer, and expressing gratitude. This means nurturing and cultivating these relationships, learning to listen, reaching out, and reminding these special friends and family members how much they mean to us as often as possible.

Expose yourself to the things and people that inspire you

As well as spending more time around the people that lift you up, seek to be someone who lifts others up too. Create a master list of all of the people and things that make you happy. Don't stop at just a few. Give it time and keep writing. You'll find this is a profound exercise for getting to know yourself better.

Learn, explore, discover

Learning affects various spheres of your life and improves quality of life. Learn new skills, read books, get informed about things happening around you, and put knowledge into action. Knowledge is the key to unlocking many doors. Advancement in your education can also lead to progress in your career.

Surround yourself with art and nature

The ability to see beauty in art and in the nature that surrounds us is very important for improving quality of life. Art is the fruit of human culture. It's more than just an aesthetic work. Each work of art also contains the essence of humanity. Nature heals the soul. Inspires it. Stills it. And rejuvenates it. Time spent in nature can restore you to a place of wholeness, calm, and clarity. Find what you like the most: forests, mountains, beaches, deserts, or gardens. The more we focus on what is good about our lives – those things that truly bring us joy – the more our joy expands.

Pay attention to the details of your home

The things that surround you can create a special atmosphere and bring positive energy to your everyday environment. What you select and what brings you harmony and joy are absolutely your choice and down to your own individual taste. It's all in the details. Think about candles, lights, music, etc. Make little places in your home a retreat. Maybe in the living room, you could have a cozy corner set up with books, plump pillows, and soft throw blankets. Or perhaps in the bathroom, you could have a table with magazines, mints, and pretty soaps. What do you really love about hotels, resorts, and spas? How can you replicate that at home? Some people will appreciate being surrounded by fresh flowers. Don't keep your best silver and china hidden in a cabinet out of the way. Use it! Treat yourself as your best guest. It's all about finding the little luxuries in life.

Take a pause (sabbatical or career break)

Have you ever considered taking time out to see life from a different perspective or living in a different country to find new inspiration, energy, and creativity? A sabbatical is when you take some time away from your job and then return to it with the blessing of your employer, sometimes even without losing your income stream if the organization is very supportive of the idea. A career break is when you resign and change direction completely. Perhaps you want to change something in your life, start a new career path, or set up your own business. You may need time to reflect, plan, decide, or learn new skills in order to achieve this. The reason people take this kind of break is to gain new experiences and qualities in life, explore new things, to learn new skills, recharge the body, and get some freedom, fun, energy, and adventure. Taking a break from your busy life is an exceptional way to connect and strengthen family bonds, enjoy more time together, and appreciate special moments. It's a unique opportunity to upgrade your quality of life by taking time to gain clarity, energy, and motivation. Do it when you are still fit enough and have the energy to absorb new cultures, meet new people, and experience daily life in a different environment.

Quality life goes far beyond how much money you have in your bank account or how many luxury items you have in your closet. Instead, it's about elevating the ordinary. It's about all the little things you can do to create a life that you find comfortable and pleasurable. As Tony Robbins (motivational speaker, author, philanthropist, and life and business strategist) said: "Happiness and success in life are not the result of what we have, but rather of how we live. What we do with the things we have makes the biggest difference in the quality of life."

In today's world, quality of life is really a state of mind. Of course, having nice things, living in a comfortable setting, having the time and money to do the things you would otherwise be unable to do and see, and having what you need at hand when you need it are all luxuries. On the other hand, if you could have a stress-free life, the spare time to do what you want, and good friends around you, then you would probably prefer to enjoy the very life you are living rather than always living for what you could have.

FINDING INNER BALANCE

There is not one simple formula for improving your quality of life. Only you know what will work best for you. Only you can change your mood, relationships, self-care, and life for the better. So much in life is outside our control, but there is also a lot within our control if we just make time to reflect and act on it. As poet Emily Dickinson said: "Find ecstasy in life, the mere sense of living is joy enough." So, today, choose to do one small thing that makes your life better.

SUMMARY

In this chapter, you have contemplated the relationship between lifestyle and quality of life. You have learned various strategies to enhance your quality of life. Again, your choices and your mindset determine how you want to live and what is truly important to you. Not everyone needs to dine off silver plates, surround themselves with fresh flowers, and have an ocean view. But, if you know how to celebrate every moment in life, cherish your time, and surround yourself with things and people that inspire you, you set yourself up to live a life full of color and simply enjoy it.

REDO INNER BALANCE INVENTORY QUESTION

In three to six months, perhaps having applied some of the strategies learned in this chapter, go back and reassess the inner balance inventory question. Ask yourself: how satisfied are you with the quality of your lifestyle and your living space? Who and what do you surround yourself with? Do you celebrate the important moments in your life?

Write your rating and reflection here. Try not to make judgments, but an honest assessment of your quality of life.

Rating on a scale of 1 to 10, with 1 being low and 10 being high:

1   2   3   4   5   6   7   8   9   10

Reflection:

AFTERWORD

This is the final step on your roadmap. By now, you have learned a great deal about how your mindset plays a crucial role in each of the 12 areas of inner balance. Now you can enjoy taking the time to explore, experiment with, and apply the various tools and methods in this book that suit you best to help create the life you want. Be creative and imaginative, and try to find the joy in your personal journey. Bear in mind that cultivating a growth mindset could be the single most important thing you ever do in the pursuit of success. Finding balance and harmony will be a lifelong project which forces you way beyond your comfort zone. Maximize the personal, professional, and financial potential that life has to offer. This book is always there to remind you of your purpose and life vision. Keep it close at hand and return to it as many times as you need, especially if you feel that you're straying off the path you've set yourself. Redo the inner balance inventory questions and roadmap again every year.

Below you will find a summary of each chapter to help you review all the positive things you have learned throughout this book. You can use this summary as a reminder and also revisit the chapters themselves in a modular fashion as and when you need to.

Chapter 1: Honing Your Life Vision

- You started sowing the seeds to begin your journey.
- You discovered how to formulate your life vision based on your core values.

- You were encouraged to identify the main goals that you want to accomplish, ideally corresponding with all 12 areas of inner balance.
- You were motivated to reflect and design your personal strategy based on a solid plan of which strategic choices to make and what you want to change, continue, or give up in life.

Chapter 2: Reaching Beyond Your Comfort Zone

- You learned about taking risks and pushing yourself in order to expand the opportunities available to you.
- You explored how to alter your way of thinking to create meaningful change.
- You were encouraged to move your mindset away from avoiding difficult situations towards finding different ways of acting and dealing with challenges.
- You discovered the benefits of moving into uncharted territory and trying something new.

Chapter 3: Boosting Your Creativity

- You were encouraged to adopt various tools and methods borrowed from the art world to solve complex problems.
- You were inspired to approach and experience the world with curiosity.
- You explored the seven key skills of artists Leonardo da Vinci and Pablo Picasso as useful capabilities for you to master.
- You were stimulated to change the focus of your thinking, allowing your mind to discover new options.

Chapter 4: Maximizing Your Productivity and Energy

- You learned how to adopt a positive mindset to manage your energy wisely using different techniques.
- You explored proven methods to maximize your productivity and energy levels.
- You were guided through how to create your own recipe for managing productivity and focusing your attention for a period of time without distractions.
- You were inspired by different tools to improve your performance, including Robin Sharma's 90/90/1 rule, the Eisenhower decision matrix and others.

Chapter 5: Nurturing Your Relationships

- You had the opportunity to reflect on the quality of the relationships in your life.
- You learned different techniques to master key skills such as communication, commitment, connection, and compassion to improve your relationships.
- You evaluated how much support you are getting from the people around you. You also considered how much they can trust, rely on, and have fun with you.
- You recognized that adopting a growth mindset gives you a better chance of building lasting relationships, which require you to put in effort and work through inevitable differences.

Chapter 6: Building a Meaningful Career

- You reflected on what career means to you and how, with an open mind, you can achieve more than you ever expected.
- You were encouraged to complete an annual self-diagnosis, decide what your real priorities are, and then formulate your career plan.
- You realized that work-life balance is about tough choices. This leads you to important decisions about many other aspects of your life outside your career too.
- You were inspired to explore possibilities, be open to new opportunities, and look at your career as if it were an open book.

Chapter 7: Becoming More Resilient Against Stress

- You were guided through how to reframe challenging situations, change your thoughts towards stress, and become more resilient against its effects.
- You were encouraged to apply different coping strategies, including a practical three-step exercise by Dr Srikumar Rao.
- You learned how to build up your ability to withstand adversity and bounce back from difficult life events.
- You were motivated to use reframing and resilience to resolve employee conflict, enhance problem-solving, and even reduce feelings of burnout or being overwhelmed.

Chapter 8: Taking Control of Your Health and Well-being

- You were given some strategies to adopt and experiment with in developing good habits for a healthy and fit lifestyle.
- You discovered the longevity concept designed to inspire you to

implement strategies to improve your chances of living a longer, healthier life.
- You were encouraged to maintain habits that support your mental health.
- You were urged to take personal responsibility for your body and mind.

Chapter 9: Embracing Spiritual Life

- You discovered methods to help you live in the present moment and improve your concentration level and attention span.
- You practiced observing your state of mind and bringing a conscious presence to everyday activities.
- You discovered different tools for exploring spirituality to find more meaning and purpose in life (for example, meditation, yoga, journaling, and taking breaks).
- You were guided through how to reduce worries, pain, and negative thinking by practicing breathing and gratitude, and finding solitude.

Chapter 10: Expanding Your Intellectual Capacity

- You learned how to develop intellectual curiosity and plant the seeds for your intellectual growth.
- You were encouraged to invest in yourself, constantly develop, broaden your horizons, and gain new skills.
- You were motivated to use five simple ways to expand your intellectual capabilities.
- You were given different tools to develop your curiosity and try something new intellectually to introduce yourself to new possibilities.

Chapter 11: Planning Financial Freedom

- You learned how to establish a healthy relationship with money and empower yourself to reach your goals.
- You were encouraged to form healthy financial habits and build wealth.
- You were guided through better ways to manage your finances and reduce financial stress.
- You were inspired to shape a positive "abundance" mindset and find the right balance between working, saving, and enjoying your life.

Chapter 12: Improving Your Quality of Life

- You contemplated the relationship between lifestyle and quality of life.
- You learned various strategies to enhance your quality of life.
- You discovered that your choices and mindset determine what is truly important to you and how you want to live.
- You were inspired to celebrate the important moments in your life and cherish your time.

WHERE TO GO NEXT

I'm sure that by this stage you have started to adopt a different way of thinking and already achieved a great deal. Not only is your mindset changing, but your way of life is changing for the better too. Remember, it's a process. Bear in mind that it takes time; the important thing is that you have started out on your unique journey. This book is always there for you to return to whenever needed. I encourage you to regularly come back to it and constantly strive to improve yourself. Remember, these 12 areas of inner balance are always a good starting point. You can set yourself goals and create a new vision for the next year, and many years to come.

THE ROADMAP

This roadmap is a working tool to help you commit to change and achieve optimal balance in life. Take a moment to reflect again on this roadmap. Drawing on the knowledge you have gained in each area of life throughout this book, decide what you want to accomplish. You can return to this tool as many times as you wish, but as a minimum you might find it helpful to look at it at the start of every new year.

AREA IN LIFE AND BUSINESS	OBSTACLES/ LIMITING BELIEFS	DREAM VISION
Reflect on a specific area: How do you want to experiment with this area of life? What would you like to change?	What drains you in this area physically, mentally, emotionally? What are you avoiding?	What choices do you see? What values are aligned with this?
1. Honing Your Vision of Life		
2. Reaching Beyond Your Comfort Zone		
3. Boosting Your Creativity		
4. Maximizing Your Productivity and Energy		
5. Nurturing Your Relationships		
6. Building a Meaningful Career		
7. Becoming More Resilient Against Stress		
8. Taking Control of Your Health and Well-being		
9. Embracing Spiritual Life		
10. Expanding Your Intellectual Capacity		
11. Planning Financial Freedom		
12. Improving Your Quality of Life		

DESIRED GOALS	HABITS	OUTCOME
Where will you look for inspiration? What is your opportunity?	What new habits would you like to introduce? How will you attain it?	How will you define success in this area? How will you measure it daily?

FINAL SUMMARY

Finally, here is a summary of this book's most important principles:

- Focus on the journey. See the value in it. Reread chapters as you go along. Experiment and come up with your own way of doing things. Remind yourself that you are always learning.
- Contemplate and recalibrate your life vision. Take note of what is changing in your life. What are your current aspirations and dreams? Check if they align with your underlying values.
- Push yourself to take risks and explore new opportunities from time to time.
- Take on challenges. Venture outside your comfort zone. Make mistakes and learn from them. Instead of shying away from challenges, embrace them.
- Experience the world with curiosity. Be creative in every area of your life. Trust that you can solve problems by looking at different options. Do what artists tend to do and ask: what would I do differently or the same next time? Free your mind to create, interpret, and visualize possibilities.
- Create your own recipe for managing productivity and becoming more focused. Experiment with it. Do the things you are scared of or tend to avoid at the time of day when you have the most energy.

- Constantly find ways to master key skills such as communication, commitment, connection, and compassion to maintain better relationships in your life.
- Complete a self-diagnosis every year to decide what your key priorities are and then formulate your career plan. Explore new possibilities. Be open to opportunities.
- Practice reframing and resilience skills to cope with unwanted stress and emotions.
- Implement strategies to improve your chances of living a longer, healthier life. Find space and time for rest and rejuvenation.
- Try to live in the present moment and bring a conscious presence to your everyday activities. Take good care of your mental health.
- Invest in yourself. Gain new skills and broaden your horizons. Each year, select what you want to focus on and use different methods to develop this new skill.
- Build healthy financial habits. Adopt a positive abundance mindset to achieve a good balance between working, saving, and enjoying your life.
- Cherish your time. Decide what is truly important to you. Celebrate every moment in your life.
- Replace negative thoughts and self-talk with more positive ones to build a growth mindset.
- Take this journey yourself or find a coach who can help you shape your mindset, remove roadblocks and develop strategies for overcoming crisis situations and creating sustainable growth.

Enjoy the process of finding balance and harmony.

SPECIAL ACKNOWLEDGMENTS

The seeds for the book were planted by my clients, who are very often under pressure and need the tools and strategies to navigate better in life and business, but usually lack balance and harmony in life. Thank you for constantly challenging me and pushing me to grow, explore uncharted territories, and trust in my methods and tools.

Thank you to my family for encouraging me to learn and explore the world, for entering me into the world of art and business, and for giving me the possibility of a diverse education in different places in Europe. To my husband Marek for sharing a passion for art and music, and for heartening me to grow way beyond my comfort zone.

To my production team: Paul Baillie-Lane for helping me to design and publish this book smoothly, editor Jo Fincham for the comprehensive feedback and sharpening the structure of the book, Lyndsay Oliver for finding my voice for writing this book, Kait McKie for taking the pictures, and Jo Foss for helping me take my first steps in writing and for encouraging me to create this book.

To my academic mentors: Prof. Marta Juchnowicz from the Warsaw School of Economics for academic support and the possibility of introducing the concept of changing mindset to various academic papers; Prof. Joaquim Vilà from the IESE Business School in Barcelona for discussing and researching the concept of changing mindset and encouraging me to expand this topic to create programs for executive leaders.

As I began to study the importance of changing mindset and its influence on transforming our lives, I benefited tremendously from various mentors. Special thanks to: Vishen Lakhiani for changing my perception of formal education and believing in work-life integration, for creating extraordinary programs that help people transform and perform to their highest potential; Marisa Peer for teaching me how to change my attitude, beliefs, thoughts, and language to increase my confidence and cope with rejection; Dr Srikumar Rao for helping me explore the philosophy of extreme resilience and learning how to bounce back from adversity; Robin Sharma for inspiring me to test his different methods of productivity and high energy; Tony Robbins for pushing me to take more action and to never give up; Eckhart Tolle for teaching me how to live in the present moment; Mel Robbins for coaching me how to take control of my life; Shannah Kennedy for introducing the concept of taking a pause in life and not waiting until retirement to experience the world in new ways; and to many others for my evolving, growing, and developing human self.

Thank you to my unique friends for believing in me, for sharing your wisdom, knowledge, and passion. Particularly: Kasia Frycz for being my second family and for constantly checking on my harmony and balance; Agata Dybowska for showing me how to cherish life, and for our walks&talks towards France, where we were discussing the most challenging aspects of life, and for your support and kindness while living abroad without my close family; Anita Kotla for intellectual and inspirational discussions about career growth, discovering the quality of life while drinking English tea at Kit Kempt's receptions, and for finding ways to reframe difficult situations in a positive way; Darek Jakubiak for deep psychological talks about life, noticing various aspects of individual differences, for discovering different perspectives of life and absolutely finding the humor in curious situations; Anna Włodarczyk for having courage and trust in introducing art to business, for your professional support in winning new projects and widening my horizons; Agnieszka Liszka for believing in 12 areas of life, encouraging me not to give up and being my intellectual inspiration for years; Magda Łoś for many insightful conversations about life transformations and music; Ania Mikołajczyk and Marek Niewiedział for provoking many inventive discussion about life, business and art; Marta Zawadzka for creative imagination and helping me to invent better art and business programs for leaders; Tomek Miśkiewicz for endless disputes about the quality of life and the choices to be taken to live outside ones comfort zone; Krystyna Boczkowska for opportunities to introduce the concept of inner balance to women in leadership; Kasia Doliwa-Dobrowolska for proving how mindset is critical in any aspect of life. To my dear inner circle of friends, for your support, kindness, and encouragement: Bogna Forkiewicz and Bartek Błażejowski, Kasia and Robert Kos, Ewelina and Wojtek Moskwa, Ania Sowa and Jarek Maik, Ania and Maciek Derda, Huma Qureshi, Dalila Tiab, Erin Nixon and Amanda Egan.

Special thanks to the music of Frédéric Chopin and the 18th International Chopin Piano Competition for challenging and inspiring me to write this book this year, and for my unique time living in Barcelona during the pandemic, providing the possibility to explore and experience life from a different perspective and with new colors, each day learning how to live outside my comfort zone.

Thank you all.

ABOUT THE AUTHOR

Agnieszka Wolińska-Skuza is a strategic business consultant, executive coach and mentor with over 20 years of experience in C-level consulting, human capital management and combining art with business. She has worked internationally on projects related to changing mindset and building company success and growth, as well as enhancing operational efficiency and streamlining, and designing business processes such as process optimization, corporate performance improvement and organizational design. She currently leads MasConsulting Art & Business as well as Enlightenment Business Consulting. She helps leaders to accelerate their careers and advance their mastery of creative problem-solving and strategic thinking capabilities. Holding a PhD in Economics, she regularly gives lectures on managing people, strategic management and innovation and design thinking at the Warsaw School of Economics. She recently cooperated with IESE Business School, University of Navarra in Barcelona. She runs creative training workshops and has published various research papers on experimental learning, organization agility and innovation. Through her business, she helps the companies she works with to excel, and shares her passion for developing a creative mindset and an optimal environment for energy, productivity and focus to flourish.

www.ingramcontent.com/pod-product-compliance
Lightning Source LLC
LaVergne TN
LVHW021653060526
838200LV00050B/2329